Little People, **BIG DREAMS**®

Treasury

50 Stories of Brilliant Dreamers

Frances Lincoln
Children's Books

50 Favourite Dreamers

When I was a child, I found history hard to understand, with its bombastic chapters and significant dates. But I loved listening to the little stories of those who came before me.

In every time and every place, as days, months, years and centuries have gone by, dreamers have inspired us to aim higher and to dream bigger. Their fun and hard times, their fears and hopes, their challenges and joys – all of it helped to shape the world we live in, making it a better, wiser and broader place.

You're about to meet fifty of these dreamers. But believe me when I say that there is a dreamer inside each of us, ready to write a new chapter in history. Because history is not just the study of the past – it helps us write the future, too. A future we build together every single day.

What will your dream be?

isabel

Maria Isabel Sánchez Vegara
Creator of the *Little People, BIG DREAMS* series

CONTENTS

1790–1885

Mary Shelley	8
Ada Lovelace	12
Harriet Tubman	16
Emmeline Pankhurst	20
Marie Curie	24
Mahatma Gandhi	28
Maria Montessori	32
Ernest Shackleton	36
Lucy Maud Montgomery	40
Coco Chanel	44

1885–1920

Georgia O'Keeffe	50
Agatha Christie	54
Amelia Earhart	58
Josephine Baker	62
Frida Kahlo	66
Astrid Lindgren	70
Alan Turing	74
Rosa Parks	78
Jesse Owens	82
Ella Fitzgerald	86

1920–1940

David Attenborough	92
Maya Angelou	96
Martin Luther King, Jr.	100
Audrey Hepburn	104
Anne Frank	108
Corazon Aquino	112
Jane Goodall	116

Rudolf Nureyev	120
Wilma Rudolph	124
John Lennon	128

1940–1947

Pelé	134
Bruce Lee	138
Vivienne Westwood	142
Bob Dylan	146
Stephen Hawking	150
Muhammad Ali	154
Aretha Franklin	158
Billie Jean King	162
Dolly Parton	166
David Bowie	170

1947–2003

Elton John	176
Zaha Hadid	180
Evonne Goolagong	184
Steve Jobs	188
Prince	192
Ayrton Senna	196
Jean-Michel Basquiat	200
Mindy Kaling	204
Malala Yousafzai	208
Greta Thunberg	212

THE 51st DREAMER	216
GLOSSARY	218
INDEX	220

Mary Shelley	8
Ada Lovelace	12
Harriet Tubman	16
Emmeline Pankhurst	20
Marie Curie	24
Mahatma Gandhi	28
Maria Montessori	32
Ernest Shackleton	36
Lucy Maud Montgomery	40
Coco Chanel	44

1790 - 1885

Mary Shelley

WRITER

Born – 1797, England
Died – 1851, England

Little Mary's life was always going to be something out of the ordinary. She was the child of two writers: a famous feminist, and an eccentric philosopher. It was a time of great change and amazing inventions – the Industrial Revolution had arrived, and London was centre stage!

Young Mary grew up with a love of books and learning. Her mother had died when she was just a baby, but Mary visited her grave every day. Here, she sat writing stories and reading her mother's books, which argued passionately for the rights of women. The powerful words made Mary feel brave. She dreamt of a future where women could write and make their mark on the world, just like men.

When she was still quite young, Mary met a poet called Percy Bysshe Shelley. To everyone's shock, Mary and Percy fell in love and ran away together. On a tour of Europe, they visited Switzerland, where they stayed with Lord Byron, a famous poet. One stormy night, Lord Byron challenged his guests to write a horror story. Mary didn't know where to start... But a few nights later, she had a horrifying dream about a monster made of old body parts, brought to life with an electric shock. The next morning, Mary began to write the story of *Frankenstein*. If it terrifies me, she thought, it will terrify others. And she was right!

Mary's story was published and became an instant success. Thrilling and scary, it was unlike any other books of the time – the first true work of science fiction and the greatest horror story ever told. Today, millions of readers still feel a chill when they read *Frankenstein* – a story written by a fearless girl who wrote something entirely new, and made her mark on the world.

'Beware; for I am fearless,
and therefore powerful.'

Mary Shelley

1797 — Mary Wollstonecraft Godwin is born in London at the start of the Industrial Revolution – a turning point in history.

1797 — When Mary is just eleven days old, her mother dies. Her mother, Mary Wollstonecraft, was the author of a best-selling book called *A Vindication of the Rights of Woman*.

1801 — Mary's father marries his neighbour. Mary doesn't get along with her new stepmother.

1810s — Growing up, Mary is well-educated for a girl of the time. She spends lots of time reading and writing.

1812 — Mary meets a married poet called Percy Bysshe Shelley. He is one of many writers, philosophers and scientists who visit her father.

1814 — Aged just sixteen, Mary runs away with Percy. It's a scandal! Only Claire, Mary's stepsister, stands by their side, travelling through Europe with them.

Ada Lovelace is born in London. Three months later, her father, Lord Byron, left England. Ada will grow up to become the first computer programmer.

Frankenstein is published, to great success. The book weaves together scientific discoveries with a story about the misuse of power.

Throughout the 1920s and 1930s, Mary has a successful writing career, publishing several more novels.

1815 1816 1818 1822 1820s 1851

At Lord Byron's house in Switzerland, a ghost story-writing contest inspires the eighteen-year-old Mary to write *Frankenstein*.

Percy drowns in a sailing accident. Mary returns to England with her two-year-old son – the only one of her five children who survived beyond early childhood.

Aged fifty-three, Mary dies. *Frankenstein* becomes a classic, retold over and over again in books, theatre and film.

Mary Shelley

Ada Lovelace

> **MATHEMATICIAN**
>
> Born – 1815, England
> Died – 1852, England

Little Ada was born in England to a mother who loved maths and a father who loved poetry. Ada's father left England when she was a baby and never returned, while her cold, distant mother was rarely at home. Left alone, with only a cat called Mrs Puff to keep her company, Ada's imagination soared. She dreamt up a machine with wings that could move in any direction, and excitedly wrote to tell her mother about her invention.

But Ada's mother didn't like her daughter using her imagination – what if she were to inherit her father's wildness and love of poetry? That would never do! She insisted that Ada concentrate on maths and logic, and nothing else. Luckily, Ada liked numbers. While other little girls were learning needlework and dancing, little Ada was solving mathematical problems. And as she grew up, Ada kept studying and inventing – and dreaming of where her talents might lead her.

One night, at a ball in London, Ada was introduced to a famous mathematician called Charles Babbage. While the other young ladies waltzed around the room, Ada sat listening to Mr Babbage as he told her about the large machine he was building, called a calculator. The calculator could do sums so quickly, it was like magic! Most people couldn't understand Babbage's invention, but Ada was fascinated and asked him to show her how the machine worked.

Ada and Babbage became friends, and worked on plans for a new machine. Ada wrote a code made up of numbers that would tell the calculator what to do. She didn't know it, but she had just invented the language that computers use today! And so, little Ada became the world's very first computer programmer – and the dreams of the little girl with the talent for mathematics and the big imagination took flight.

'The more I study, the more insatiable do I feel my genius for it to be.'

Augusta Ada Byron is born in London to Lady Byron, a talented mathematician, and Lord Byron, a famous poet. Lord Byron leaves his family when Ada is five weeks old.

Ada's father dies when she is eight. She never meets him.

When she is fourteen, Ada becomes sick with measles. She has to spend almost a year in bed.

1815   1820   1824   1828   1830   1833

From the age of four, Ada is taught mathematics and science – unusual for a girl at that time. Her mother is often away, so Ada is looked after by her grandmother or a governess.

Aged twelve, Ada starts to dream of flying machines. She studies the way birds fly, tests out different materials from feathers to silk, and writes down her thoughts in a book called *Flyology*.

Ada is introduced to Charles Babbage, a mathematician and inventor. He tells Ada about a large calculator he is building, called the Difference Engine.

14

Ada and Babbage become friends. He calls her his 'Enchantress of Numbers'.

At nineteen, Ada marries William King. He later becomes the Earl of Lovelace, making Ada a countess.

Ada dies, aged just thirty-six. In 1953, her notes are rediscovered, and her achievements are recognised. In 1980, the US Department of Defense name a new computer language 'Ada'.

1834 · 1834 · 1835 · 1843 · 1852 · 1940s

Ada helps Babbage develop his idea for another machine designed for more complicated calculations, called the Analytical Engine.

Ada writes an algorithm (step-by-step commands) for the Analytical Engine – the very first computer program. She correctly predicts that anything (for example, music and images) can be turned into numbers and programmed into a machine.

Almost a hundred years after Ada's death, another great British mathematician, Alan Turing, becomes the founder of modern computing.

Ada Lovelace

Harriet Tubman

ANTI-SLAVERY ACTIVIST

Born – c.1822, United States
Died – 1913, United States

Little Harriet was born into enslavement on a plantation in Maryland. Even as a small child, she was forced to work from dawn to dusk, and many days she was beaten by her white enslavers. At night, Harriet gazed up at the moon and wished that she and her family could be free. It seemed a faraway dream for the little girl. But as she grew older, Harriet became more and more determined to make that dream come true.

One night, Harriet summoned up every drop of her strength and courage, and said goodbye to her beloved family. She set off on a long, dangerous journey to the North, where enslavement no longer existed. Harriet hid in the daytime and travelled at night, guided by the Pole Star. When she crossed into the Free State of Pennsylvania, she was overcome with relief.

But Harriet wasn't content with her own freedom – she wanted others to be free, too. So, she joined the Underground Railroad, a secret network of safe houses and people that helped enslaved African-Americans reach safety in the North. Harriet returned to the South to rescue her family, and then repeated the same perilous trip again and again, guiding hundreds of people to freedom. She never lost a single one.

When Civil War broke out between the North and South, Harriet led a mission to rescue 700 enslaved people. She was a hero! The war ended slavery, and millions of people were free for the first time in their lives. But unequal rules for African Americans carried on long after, and Harriet continued to speak out and demand her rights. Because little Harriet knew that you have to use all of your strength to stand up for yourself, so that you can stand up for others, too.

'... I prayed to God to make me strong and able to fight.'

Harriet Tubman

Araminta ('Minty') is born into enslavement on a plantation in Maryland. At the time, slavery is legal in some parts of America.

As a young girl, Minty is hit on the head with a heavy weight. The injury gives her pain for the rest of her life.

Harriet joins the Underground Railway, and returns to the South to rescue some of her family.

c. 1822 | 1820s | c. 1832 | 1849 | 1850 | 1850s

From the age of five, Minty is forced to work. Her family is split apart when three of her sisters are sold to other plantations.

Minty makes a plan to escape. She changes her name to Harriet Tubman, so she can't be traced, and travels 145 km north to Philadelphia.

Over eleven years, Harriet guides hundreds of enslaved people to the safety of the Northern States and Canada. She calls the people she rescues her 'passengers'.

In the Civil War, Harriet works as a cook, nurse and spy. She frees hundreds of enslaved people in a daring mission, leading three steamboats along rivers full of explosives.

Harriet settles in Auburn, New York. She takes to the stage to demand equal rights for women and African-American people.

Rosa Parks, another great freedom fighter, is born. Like Harriet, she fights for equality for all.

1862   1865   1870s   1903   1913   1913

When the Civil War ends, slavery is finally abolished. There is a great celebration!

An elderly Harriet gives some of her land to a church in Auburn. The Harriet Tubman Home for the Aged opens here in 1908.

Harriet dies. She remains a symbol of strength, hope and bravery for many people around the world.

Harriet Tubman

Emmeline Pankhurst

WOMEN'S RIGHTS LEADER

Born – 1858, England
Died – 1928, England

Little Emmeline was born into a prominent family of activists in Manchester. Inspired by literature, she dreamed of being a great hero. But at that time, women had very few rights compared to men, so she couldn't pursue her dreams. Even though her parents believed that women should have the right to vote, or suffrage, she was denied the same education as her brothers because she was a girl. It was hard for her to understand why.

Emmeline soon realised that denying rights to women was a much bigger problem than her own dreams. After attending a meeting with her mother, she learned that women needed to vote in order to improve terrible conditions in society. She knew what she had to do; she would devote her life to suffrage. When she met fellow suffragist Richard Pankhurst, they fell in love. They married and raised their children while fighting for women's rights.

After Richard's death, Emmeline began a new suffrage group with her daughters. Their members became known as Suffragettes. They held rallies and protests, shouted in the streets and vandalised buildings to bring attention to their cause. Politicians, police and the public fought against them. Many Suffragettes were imprisoned, including Emmeline and her daughter, Christabel. Others were injured or killed. But Emmeline led the Suffragettes to face discomfort and never, ever give up.

When World War One broke out in Europe, Suffragettes took jobs left behind by men. They showed the world that a woman could do any job as well as a man. Finally, some women were granted the right to vote in the UK. Emmeline didn't live to see full suffrage, but her dream of being a hero had come true. Her selfless and bold activism inspired successful suffrage movements and still inspires feminists of all generations to keep up the fight for true equality.

'There can be no peace in the world until woman is given liberty in the councils of the world.'

Emmeline Pankhurst

1858 — Emmeline is born. By age four, she is reading. She often reads the newspapers to her father over breakfast.

1874 — Emmeline weds activist Richard Pankhurst. Together, they raise a family and fight to make progress for the suffrage movement.

1898 — When Richard dies unexpectedly, Emmeline is devastated. As an unmarried woman, she has few options to earn money and support her family. She must find a job and raise her children, but she keeps fighting for suffrage.

1879 — Emmeline begs her mother to bring her to a speech by suffragist Lydia Becker. She leaves the meeting with her life purpose.

1894 — Emmeline works for public assistance, and sees that women in her society withstand terrible treatment at work and home, without any rights to change it.

1903 — Frustrated by ineffective suffrage groups, Emmeline and her daughters form the Women's Social and Political Union. Their motto is 'Deeds, not words.'

Emmeline and the Suffragettes protest at Downing Street and Buckingham Palace.

Emmeline tours the US and Canada to raise money for suffrage.

The first suffrage bill passes, allowing only women over 30 who own property the right to vote. This was the first step toward winning women their rightful place in public life.

1905 1908 1909 1917 1918 1928

Emmeline is arrested and imprisoned for protesting.

Emmeline and Christabel change the WSPU into a political party called the Women's Party. Christabel runs for office as the first female parliamentary candidate and loses in a very close race.

Emmeline dies. Later that year, full suffrage is granted to all women in the UK, regardless of race, class or status.

Emmeline Pankhurst

Marie Curie

SCIENTIST

Born – 1867, Poland
Died – 1934, France

Little Marie was a remarkable child, with an incredible love of learning. At school, she was a brilliant student and won a gold medal for her studies, which she kept in her drawer like a treasure. Marie didn't want to be a princess – she dreamt of being a scientist!

In Poland, where Marie lived, only men were allowed to study at university. But Marie didn't let this stop her. Life isn't easy, she thought, but I believe in myself and I won't give up. For five long years she worked to save enough money to study at the famous Sorbonne University in France. Studying in a new language wasn't easy, and Marie was so poor she survived on buttered bread and tea, but soon she became one of the best maths and science students in Paris.

Marie met Pierre, who loved science just as much as she did. They married and worked side by side in their laboratory. Here, Marie became fascinated by radioactivity – the rays that some chemical elements give off. Soon, Marie and Pierre discovered something incredible: two new elements, radium and polonium! It was a thrilling moment for science, and Marie and Pierre won a Nobel Prize in Physics for their research.

Marie's world turned upside down when her beloved Pierre was killed in a road accident. She wiped her tears away… and worked harder than ever. The audience applauded loudly the day she was awarded her second Nobel Prize – this time for Chemistry. Many girls followed in her footsteps, studying at her Parisian institute. Marie had valuable advice for every new student: in life, there is nothing to be afraid of, only many things to learn, and many ways to help those in need.

'Nothing in life is to be feared,
it is only to be understood.'

Marie Curie

Marie Curie is born Maria Salomea Skłodowska in Warsaw, Poland, the youngest of five children. Her parents are both teachers.

Maria isn't allowed to go to the same university as her brother because she is a girl. She saves up money by working as a teacher and a governess, and reads science books in her spare time.

Marie meets Pierre Curie. They marry the following year, and have two daughters.

1867   1870s   c.1886   1891   1894   1898

Maria (third from left) learns to read and write at a young age. She overcomes the loss of her mother at the age of ten to become a brilliant student.

Aged twenty-three, Maria moves to Paris, France. She changes her name to Marie to fit in, and studies physics and mathematics at Sorbonne University.

The Curies announce the discovery of two new elements, polonium and radium. They name polonium after Marie's homeland, Poland.

The Nobel Prize in Physics is awarded to Marie, Pierre and a man named Henri Becquerel, for their work in radiation. Marie is the first woman to win the prize.

Marie wins a second Nobel Prize, for Chemistry. She is the only person, ever, to win the prize in two different sciences.

Marie's oldest daughter, Irène, works as her mother's assistant at the Radium Institute. Irène goes on to win a Nobel Prize in Chemistry, in 1935.

1903 1906 1911 1914 1920s 1934

When Pierre dies, Marie throws herself into her research. She becomes the first woman physics professor at the Sorbonne. Three years later, she founds the Radium Institute, where research and teaching takes place.

When World War One breaks out, Marie's discoveries in radiation are used by doctors to help treat injured soldiers. She creates mobile X-ray machines that can be driven to battlefield hospitals. The trucks are called *petites Curies* ('little Curies').

Marie dies, of a disease caused by radiation. Today, her groundbreaking discoveries continue to help people with illnesses all around the world.

Marie Curie

Mahatma Gandhi

CIVIL RIGHTS LEADER

Born – 1869, India
Died – 1948, India

Little Mohandas grew up in a city by the Indian coast. Even as a young boy, he thought deeply about what was right and wrong. From his mother, he learnt values he would keep all his life, such as never harming another living thing. The shy, warm-hearted little boy dreamt of a world where people were treated equally and with kindness.

At that time, the British Empire ruled India, and when Mohandas was nineteen, he travelled to London to study law. Later, he moved to South Africa for work, as many Indians did. Things were not easy for Indians there. One day, Mohandas was thrown out of a train for refusing to leave first class – a carriage that was reserved for white people only. Mohandas decided to protest against this injustice in his own gentle way. He sat quietly in the middle of the street. Soon, thousands of Indians joined him. It was the first non-violent resistance movement ever.

Mohandas returned to India, leading a peaceful movement to free the country from British rule. To show support to his people, he took off his expensive suit and started wearing traditional Indian clothes. His supporters protested against unfair British laws by refusing to work, wear British-made clothes or set foot in British courts or schools. Mohandas was put in jail many times for organising these protests, but he never wavered from his dream of a free India, where everyone would live in peace and be treated fairly. His people called him 'Mahatma', meaning 'great soul'.

India eventually won its independence from Britain, and Mahatma became the father of the Indian nation. And the little boy with the big heart, who became a famous leader for civil rights, proved that sometimes, the power of peace is greater than the power of force.

'In a gentle way, you can shake the world.'

Mahatma Gandhi

Mohandas Gandhi is born in Porbandar, India. At the time, India is ruled by Britain.

Nineteen-year-old Gandhi sets sail to London, England, to study law.

Gandhi moves to South Africa. For twenty years, he works to improve the rights of Indians in South Africa, using a form of peaceful protest that becomes known as 'satyagraha', meaning 'holding onto truth'.

1869   1870s   1888   1891   1893   1915

Gandhi grows up with the religions of Hinduism and Jainism. One of Jainism's main ideas is a commitment to non-violence.

Gandhi returns to India and starts his own law practice, but it isn't a success – in his first courtroom case, he is so nervous he runs away!

Gandhi returns to India to lead the movement to end British rule.

Gandhi starts to wear traditional Indian clothes – the same clothes that poor people wear.

When Britain makes salt too expensive to buy, Gandhi leads Indians on a 241-mile march to the Indian Ocean to harvest their own.

India gains its independence from Britain. It is split into two independent nations: India (mainly Hindu) and Pakistan (mainly Muslim).

1921 1920s 1930 1942 1947 1948

From the 1920s onwards, Gandhi organises many non-violent protests, and is jailed several times.

Gandhi is arrested when he calls for Indian independence. He is released nineteen months later – the British are scared the country will riot if he is left in prison.

Gandhi is shot and killed by a man who disagrees with his call for peace between religions. He is remembered as a passionate hero who fought for freedom and opposed violence at all costs.

Mahatma Gandhi

Maria Montessori

DOCTOR AND EDUCATOR

Born – 1870, Italy
Died – 1952, Netherlands

Little Maria was born with an incredible will to learn. And of everything she learnt, she loved maths and science best. At that time in Italy, there were very strict ideas about what girls should study – and science was not on the list. But Maria was a trailblazer from the very beginning. She dreamt of choosing her own path in life. If the only way to study science was at an all-boys school, then that's where she would have to go. And she did!

Maria decided to become a doctor. Despite all the obstacles in her way, she made it to university and became the first girl in Italy to study medicine. It wasn't easy – the male students looked down on her, and she was sometimes forced to study alone. But she didn't give up.

Maria became a doctor in a hospital, where children with learning disabilities were stuck in a bare room and treated as if they were ill. This can't be right, Maria thought. So, she chose to give the children love and attention as part of their treatment. She reasoned that if the children believed in themselves, they would flourish. And she was right. By using fun activities and games, the children started to learn through play.

Maria realised her idea could work with any child. She opened a school called the Children's House, where children were encouraged to play and follow their own interests. Instead of sitting in desks before a teacher, they were given the freedom to explore tables full of counting beads and puzzles. The children made amazing progress.

Maria wrote many books, and travelled the world teaching her revolutionary method. Many schools, orphanages and nurseries followed in her footsteps – from Italy to America and India. And little Maria, who always chose her own path, inspired children to be free, curious and responsible human beings, just like her.

'Never help a child with a task at which he feels he can succeed.'

Maria Montessori

Maria Montessori is born in Chiaravalle, in Italy.

As a teenager, Maria studies mathematics and science at an all-boys technical school.

At the International Congress for Women in Berlin, Maria argues that women should be paid the same as men.

1870 1876 1886 1893 1896 1897

In Rome, Maria goes to the local state school, where she invents games to make learning more fun.

With her mother's support, Maria becomes the first woman in Italy to go to medical school.

Maria starts working as an assistant doctor with children with learning disabilities. They blossom in her care.

Maria sets up a school for children with learning disabilities. She does lots of research to see how children learn and develop.

Maria's first book is published – it becomes a bestseller! The ideas in Maria's book will be used around the world.

Little Anne Frank, the famous schoolgirl diarist, spends six years at a Montessori school in the Netherlands.

1900   1907   1909   1913   1930s   1952

Maria expands her ideas to all children. Her first Casa dei Bambini or 'Children's House' opens.

Maria begins to travel around the world, giving courses and lectures. She continues to travel and teach until her death.

Maria dies, but the legacy of her work continues today in Montessori schools around the world.

Maria Montessori

Ernest Shackleton

> **EXPLORER**
>
> Born – 1874, Ireland
> Died – 1922, South Georgia

Little Ernest always longed for adventure. His father wanted him to become a doctor, but Ernest had other ideas. He wanted to be an explorer! He dreamt of travelling far, far away... further than anyone had ever gone before.

Ernest left school to join the merchant navy, longing to become the first person to reach the South Pole – the southernmost place on Earth. Twice, he joined expeditions trying to reach it, and twice he came tantalizingly close, but Roald Amundsen, a Norwegian explorer, got there first. So, Ernest planned a new feat: to cross Antarctica from sea to sea, via the South Pole. It would be the greatest journey ever attempted!

In August 1914, a team of 28 men, 69 sled dogs and a cat named Mrs Chippy headed to Antarctica on a ship called the *Endurance*. As they sailed south, the ice closed in, and their ship became trapped. Nine long, bitterly cold months passed, and the ice started slowly crushing the ship. If the men stayed, they would die.

Ernest summoned all his courage and set himself a new task: saving his crew. He led his exhausted, frozen men across the ice, dragging three heavy lifeboats, to the open ocean. After many days at sea, they finally reached Elephant Island – an uninhabited outcrop. Realising there was little hope of rescue here, Ernest set off with five men on another long, treacherous journey across the ocean to South Georgia, where they found help at a whaling station. The rest of Ernest's crew were rescued three months later. Everybody thought it was a miracle! But Ernest never lost faith in bringing his men home.

Little Ernest lived through one of the most incredible adventures of all time. Today, his optimism, perseverance and courage inspire dreamers and adventurers everywhere.

'Difficulties are just things to overcome after all.'

Ernest Shackleton

Ernest Henry Shackleton is born in the Irish county of Kildare. He grows up on a farm, the second of ten children.

At sixteen, Ernest leaves school to join the merchant navy. By the age of twenty-four, he is a master mariner.

Ernest returns to Antarctica as leader of his own expedition, aboard the *Nimrod*. This time, he gets to within 180 km of the South Pole! On his return to Britain, he is knighted.

1874　1884　1890　1901　1908　1911

The family move to London when Ernest is ten. His father sends him to the prestigious Dulwich College.

Ernest goes on his first expedition to Antarctica, aboard the *Discovery*. His journey by sledge over the ice takes him closer to the South Pole than anyone before – under 800 km.

When Norwegian explorer Roald Amundsen reaches the South Pole, Ernest sets himself a new goal: to cross Antarctica via the South Pole.

Ernest and his crew set out from London aboard the *Endurance*.

The crew set off in three small boats, reaching Elephant Island after seven days. Ernest and five men set off to find help in South Georgia, crossing 1,300 km of ocean in sixteen days. All of Ernest's crew are later rescued. He is a hero!

Ernest's book about the *Endurance* expedition, called *South*, is published.

1914   1915   1916   1917   1919   1922

By early 1915, the ship is trapped, and Ernest's crew are forced to live on the floating ice. Ernest keeps spirits up by organising dog races and football games.

During World War One, Ernest serves in the British army.

Ernest plans a fourth expedition, to circumnavigate Antarctica, but he dies in South Georgia before the ship sets sail.

Ernest Shackleton

Lucy Maud Montgomery

> **WRITER**
>
> Born – 1874, Canada
> Died – 1942, Canada

Little Maud had a lonely childhood. She was born on Prince Edward Island, in Canada, and when she was very small, her mother died. Maud's father left his daughter in the care of her grandparents and sailed away, leaving the island far behind. Poor Maud got little affection from her grandparents, who were strict and bad-tempered. But she loved to roam around the island, picking berries and naming everything she saw, even the apple trees! Books, paper and pens became Maud's best friends. Her grandparents thought reading and writing were a waste of time, especially for a girl. But Maud could no more stop writing than breathing. At night, she smuggled candles into her room to write in secret, dreaming of one day becoming an author.

When Maud was older, she started teaching at a school on the island, and wrote in her spare time. Soon, one of her stories was published in a magazine, and then another, and another! Before long, dozens of her stories had been printed. One day, Maud came across an interesting story in an old newspaper: 'Elderly couple apply to orphan asylum for a boy. By mistake, a girl is sent to them.' That night, Maud dreamt of the little orphan girl... and the following day she decided to make her the star of her next story, *Anne of Green Gables*.

When the book was published, it was an instant success. Everyone loved Anne, the little girl with freckles and thick red braids. She was imaginative and brave, and though she got into scrapes, she was always loved. Through Anne's adventures, Maud rewrote her own childhood as she'd have liked it to be. And by telling Anne's story, Maud – the little girl who wasn't allowed to write – became the great author she always dreamt she could be.

'Isn't it nice to think that tomorrow is a new day with no mistakes in it yet?'

Lucy Maud Montgomery

| 1874 | 1876 | 1881 | 1887 | 1891 | 1894 |

Lucy Maud Montgomery is born on Prince Edward Island, in Canada. She later decides she prefers to be called Maud.

From the age of six, Maud attends the local one-room school. She starts writing poetry and journals when she is nine.

Maud's first piece of writing is published – a poem in a Prince Edward Island newspaper.

When Maud is twenty-one months old, her mother dies. Her father moves to the mainland, sending Maud to live with her grandparents.

Aged thirteen, Maud writes in her diary about her dream of being famous and becoming 'the wonder of my schoolmates – a little local celebrity'.

Maud qualifies as a teacher and starts work at a school on the island.

| 1897 | 1898 | 1905 | 1907 | 1911 | 1942 |

1897 — Maud's first short story is published. Over the next ten years, she has over a hundred stories published in magazines and newspapers.

1905 — Maud writes *Anne of Green Gables*. After many rejections by publishers, the book is finally published in 1908, and is a huge success – children everywhere love it!

1911 — Maud gets married and leaves King Edward Island. Over the next thirty years she continues writing short stories, poems and novels – many of them set on the island.

1898 — When her grandfather dies, Maud has to return home to care for her grandmother. She lives with her for most of the next thirteen years.

1907 — In Sweden, another great children's book writer is born – Astrid Lindgren, author of *Pippi Longstocking*.

1942 — Maud dies, aged sixty-seven. The world mourns the author who created one of the best-loved characters in children's literature.

Lucy Maud Montgomery

Coco Chanel

FASHION DESIGNER

Born – 1883, France
Died – 1971, France

Little Coco always stood out from the crowd. At the strict orphanage where she lived, poor Coco found it impossible to follow the rules – she'd rather make her own. While the other girls played with toys, Coco sewed beautiful dresses for her dolls. She dreamt that one day, she would wear beautiful clothes herself.

When she left the orphanage, Coco worked as a seamstress by day, and sang on stage at night! Who said she couldn't do both? Tumbling into bed late at night, she dreamt of all the things she wanted to do. Coco started making hats for her friends, and soon opened her own hat shop. The mademoiselles of Paris loved Coco's modern, simple designs, so different to the fussy styles they were used to.

One day, Coco was struck by a new thought. Why was it, she wondered, that men wore comfortable clothes that were easy to move around in, while women had to put up with billowing petticoats and tight corsets? It didn't seem right. One day, Coco sewed herself a dress from some soft and stretchy fabric. The style was bold and different – too different for some people. But her friends liked it so much that Coco made more and more dresses. Her simple, elegant designs allowed women the same freedom and comfort as men. Soon, her rule-breaking creations became a sensation!

Coco opened a fashion house in Paris. Artists, actors, writers and singers all had to have the latest Chanel designs. Women were inspired to cut their hair short and wear trousers, just like Coco. The little girl who had once longed for beautiful clothes had become a worldwide fashion icon by doing things her own way. Coco Chanel remains one of the greatest fashion designers in history: the rebellious girl with an eye for style and simplicity, who changed women's clothing forever.

'In order to be irreplaceable one must always be different.'

Coco Chanel

Gabrielle Chanel is born in a poorhouse in Saumur, France.

Gabrielle leaves school and gets a job as a seamstress. In the evenings, she sings on the stage. The soldiers in the audience nickname her 'Coco' — the name of a lost dog in one of her songs.

Coco begins to design clothes as well as hats, and opens her first boutique. Her clothes are loose, easy-to-wear and elegant. 'Luxury must be comfortable, otherwise it is not luxury,' she says.

1883 1894 1901 1909 1913 1918

After her mother dies, Gabrielle is sent to live in an orphanage, where she is taught how to sew by the nuns.

Coco opens a hat shop in Paris. Her simple, elegant designs are a big hit with famous actresses and society ladies.

Coco opens a couture house in 31 Rue Cambon, a fashionable district of Paris.

The first Chanel perfume is launched, bringing Coco fame around the world. It's called Chanel No. 5 because Coco chose the fifth perfume sample shown to her, after a fortune teller told her five was her lucky number.

Coco closes her couture house when World War Two breaks out. It stays closed for fifteen years.

In her seventies, when most people have stopped work, Coco decides to relaunch her career. Her designs are as popular as ever.

1921   1926   1939   1941   1954   1971

Coco designs the iconic 'little black dress', taking a colour associated with sadness and making it the height of fashion.

Another great fashion designer, Vivienne Westwood, is born.

Coco dies in Paris, but her influence on women's fashion continues. She is the only fashion designer included in *TIME* magazine's list of the 100 most important people of the 20th century.

Coco Chanel

47

Georgia O'Keeffe

Agatha Christie

Amelia Earhart

Josephine Baker

Frida Kahlo

Astrid Lindgren

Alan Turing

Rosa Parks

Jesse Owens

Ella Fitzgerald

1885 – 1920

Georgia O'Keeffe

> **PAINTER**
> Born – 1887, United States
> Died – 1986, United States

Little Georgia saw the beauty in the world from the moment she was born. While other children played games, she entertained herself with the big blue sky and wide-open prairie around the family farm in Wisconsin. For her, every stone and flower was worth looking at. Other people would call those things ordinary, but not Georgia. She dreamt of a world where everyone could see the wonder in each day.

By the time she was twelve, Georgia knew that she was going to be an artist. She took art lessons, and later went to art school. Slowly, she began to develop her own style, something that was entirely new. She didn't just want to show how things looked, but how they made her feel. When a friend showed some of her drawings to a photographer, Alfred Stieglitz, he loved them! An exhibition of Georgia's art was held at Alfred's gallery in New York, and people were amazed.

Georgia and Alfred fell in love and got married. Inspired by New York, Georgia carried on painting. It made her sad that people in the city were too busy to notice the beauty in the little things around them. So, Georgia decided to make those little things big! She painted flowers that filled whole canvasses, so that no one could ignore them. 'I will make even busy New Yorkers take time to see what I see of flowers,' she said.

When summer came, Georgia visited New Mexico, and fell in love with the wild desert landscape. She painted crosses, sand dunes and even the skulls of dead animals. People loved Georgia's paintings and they were shown all around the world. The little girl who noticed the small things became the painter who taught us that the ordinary becomes extraordinary, when you just take the time to look at it.

'To create one's own world takes courage.'

Georgia O'Keeffe

Georgia is born on a farm in Sun Prairie, Wisconsin, and grows up with six brothers and sisters.

Georgia moves to Chicago, and later to New York City, to study art.

Alfred Stieglitz exhibits Georgia's exciting new art at his gallery in New York City. It helps catapult her to success.

1887   1900s   1905   1912   1917   1924

As a teenager, Georgia has art lessons, and spends her spare time painting with her grandmother and sisters.

While working as an art teacher, Georgia begins to develop her own style. Her drawings use shapes and lines to express her feelings about objects. They are very different to the American art of the time.

Alfred and Georgia marry. During their marriage, they write over 25,000 letters to each other, sometimes as many as two or three a day!

Georgia starts painting huge, close-up paintings of flowers. Later, she paints New York skyscrapers. By 1927, she's one of the most important artists in America.

Georgia buys a crumbling house in the village of Abiquiú, in New Mexico.

In the 1950s and 1960s, Georgia travels the world, finding new inspiration for her paintings, but she always returns home to New Mexico.

1925 1929 1940 1949 1950s 1986

Georgia first visits New Mexico and falls in love with the culture and landscape. She begins to spend part of every year there, painting everything from red hills to animal bones.

After Alfred dies, Georgia moves to New Mexico permanently.

Georgia dies, at the age of ninety-nine. She is remembered as one of the most influential and remarkable painters of the 20th century.

Georgia O'Keeffe

Agatha Christie

WRITER

Born – 1890, England
Died – 1976, England

To little Agatha, the real world was never as exciting as her imagination. Left to her own company as a child, Agatha invented imaginary friends, had long conversations with her dog and spent hours curled up with a book. Detective stories were her favourite. There was not a single doubt in Agatha's mind that when she grew up, she would be a writer. She dreamt that one day it would be *her* name on the front cover.

When war broke out, Agatha put her books aside and went to work at a hospital, looking after wounded soldiers and dispensing medicines. But her imagination wouldn't stay quiet. Sitting on the tram, she imagined the other passengers were characters in a story – villains, victims, perhaps even a famous detective! As a nurse, she learnt about fascinating poisons and toxic potions that could cause someone to meet a sticky end...

Agatha began to write a new story, which started with the mysterious murder of a rich heiress. Who could solve such a terrible crime? Agatha invented Hercule Poirot, a detective with a magnificent moustache and a head exactly the shape of an egg. Soon, Agatha proudly held a newly printed book in her hands – with her name on the cover!

Carrying her typewriter, Agatha journeyed around the world. As she travelled, she found inspiration for her stories. People read with wonder as first Poirot, and then a new detective, the elderly Miss Marple, solved thrilling crime after crime. And the little girl who dreamt of seeing her name in print became the best-selling novelist of all time. Agatha wrote more than a hundred books, but she was always pondering her next mystery... Luckily, Agatha knew that any mystery can be solved if you use your imagination.

'The best time to plan a book is when you're doing the dishes.'

Agatha Christie

Agatha Mary Clarissa Miller is born in 1890 in Devon, England. She is the youngest of three children.

When World War One breaks out, Agatha works at the local hospital. She gets married the same year to Archie Christie.

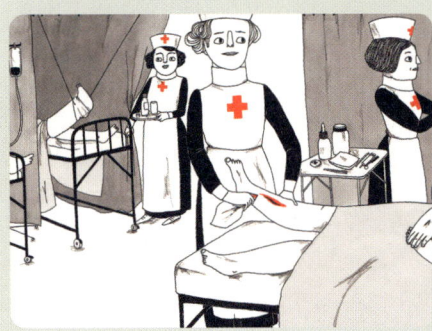

With her husband and her typewriter, Agatha travels across the British Empire. In Hawaii, she becomes the first woman in the West to learn how to surf standing up!

1890 1890s 1914 1920 1922 1926

Agatha is educated at home. By age five, she has taught herself to read, and at eighteen she is writing short stories.

Agatha's first book, *The Mysterious Affair at Styles*, is published. It introduces the world to the Belgian detective, Hercule Poirot.

Agatha inspires her own mystery when she disappears, leading to a nationwide hunt. She is eventually found safe and sound in a hotel.

Inspired by a trip on the Orient Express train, Agatha writes one of her most famous novels, *Murder on the Orient Express*.

In the 1930s and 1940s, Agatha travels with her new husband Max, an archaeologist, and writes two or three books a year.

Agatha meets Queen Elizabeth II at the film premiere of *Murder on the Orient Express*. She likes the film, but complains that Poirot's moustache isn't luxuriant enough!

1928 1930 1930s 1952 1974 1976

Murder at the Vicarage is published, featuring a new investigator, the elderly Miss Jane Marple. Soon all of Agatha's readers love Miss Marple as much as Poirot.

One of Agatha's plays, *The Mousetrap*, opens at a London theatre. It becomes the world's longest-running play.

At the age of eighty-five, Agatha dies – the top-selling author in history. Her books have sold more than two billion copies and been translated into more than a hundred languages.

Agatha Christie

Amelia Earhart

> **AVIATOR**
>
> Born – 1897, United States
> Disappeared – 1937, Pacific Ocean

Little Amelia liked to collect insects, climb trees and race her sledge as fast as it would go, imagining she was flying like a bird. When she was older, Amelia visited an air show, and watched the planes soar and swoop in the sky. How she longed to be up there with them! A little later, she got her first ride in a plane. From that moment on, she dreamt of being a pilot.

Amelia took lessons, cut her hair short and bought a bright yellow plane, which she nicknamed 'The Canary'. After months of practising, she became the first woman to fly up to 4,267 metres. Later, she was invited to be the first woman to fly over the Atlantic Ocean as a passenger. The flight made her famous, but Amelia knew that women could fly planes just as well as men. She decided to repeat the journey, but this time all by herself. Taking off from Canada, Amelia's little red plane flew over the vast, empty ocean, landing fourteen hours later in a field in Ireland – she had done it! Amelia was a hero around the world.

Amelia went on to break many more flying records. As her fortieth birthday approached, she decided she wanted a new challenge: to fly around the world. Some people said the journey was crazy, but Amelia wasn't afraid of adventures. She and her navigator flew for thousands of miles, over stormy oceans and steamy jungles, until they reached the middle of the Pacific Ocean. Here, Amelia sent a radio message that their fuel was running low. Soon afterwards, all communications from the plane stopped. Amelia and her plane had vanished. The world mourned Amelia, the little girl who wanted to soar like a bird, who showed the world how high women can fly.

'You can do anything you decide to do.'

Amelia Earhart

Amelia Earhart is born in Kansas, USA.

At this time, women around the world did not have the same rights or opportunities as men. Over in England, Emmeline Pankhurst is campaigning for equal rights for women.

Pilot Frank Hawks gives Amelia her first ride in a biplane. From that moment on, she says, 'I knew I had to fly'.

1897 1900s 1910s 1918 1920 1921

Growing up, Amelia climbs trees, collects frogs and learns to shoot a rifle. When she is six, the Wright brothers make the world's first aeroplane flight.

Amelia first becomes interested in planes after seeing an air show.

Amelia takes flying lessons, buys her first plane and sets a new women's world record by flying up to 14,000 feet. In 1923, she gains an international pilot's licence – one of only sixteen women in the world to have one.

Amelia is invited to take part in a historic flight across the Atlantic Ocean, with a pilot and a mechanic. On her return, she is famous!

Amelia flies solo across the Atlantic Ocean. The flight is dangerous, with bad weather and mechanical difficulties, but she makes it!

Amelia decides to try and fly 46,000 km around the world. She and Fred Noonan, her navigator, set off from Florida on June 1st.

1928 1929 1932 1935 1937 1937

To support female flying, Amelia founds the Ninety-Nines, a club with ninety-nine female pilots.

Amelia becomes the first person to fly solo across the Pacific Ocean, from Hawaii to California.

On July 2nd, Amelia and Fred are trying to reach Howland Island in the mid-Pacific, when their plane vanishes. A huge rescue attempt is launched, but Amelia is never found.

Amelia Earhart

Josephine Baker

> **PERFORMER, SPY AND ACTIVIST**
> Born – 1906, United States
> Died – 1975, France

Some might say little Josephine was born with nothing, but she had two legs made for dancing, a dazzling smile and a dream to be one of the biggest and brightest stars the world had ever seen. When Josephine was young, there were separate rules for Black and white people in America. 'Segregation' meant Black people weren't allowed to go to the same schools or eat in the same places as white people, and weren't treated equally in American society. Josephine wasn't happy with that. She had dreams to live her life as a person equal to any other. Dancing her way out of St Louis to New York City, she wowed audiences with moves that were somehow silly and stylish at the same time.

Josephine soon felt she had gone as far as a Black woman could go in America at that time. She moved to Paris, and for the first time in her life she felt free. She became an overnight star, meeting famous writers, artists and actors. People in Europe were thrilled with her exciting dances – the shimmy, the moosh, the messaround and the Charleston. During World War Two, Josephine was quick to offer her help. She performed for American and French troops and worked as a spy, smuggling secret messages in her music sheets. She was a hero of the French Resistance!

With times beginning to change in America, Josephine returned to the country, marching and speaking up for equal rights. She became an important part of America's Civil Rights Movement that ended segregation. When she celebrated her fifty-year career on stage, little Josephine, with the fantastic dance moves and big heart, who fought so hard to be in a world that would accept her as an equal, performed to standing ovations. She wept with joy.

'... the people of the world can learn to live together in peace if they are not brought up in prejudice.'

Josephine Baker

Josephine is born in St Louis, Missouri, and raised by her mother.

Josephine moves to New York City and begins performing in Broadway shows, impressing theatre-goers with her skilled and often comic dancing.

One year after arriving in Paris, Josephine is one of the highest-paid and most popular performers in Europe.

1906 **1919** **1923** **1925** **1926** **1927**

Leaving home aged thirteen, Josephine begins dancing with a theatre group that tours the country.

Josephine sails to Paris and becomes famous almost overnight.

Josephine stars in the silent film *Siren of the Tropics*.

At the height of her fame, Josephine begins to acquire several exotic animals, including a pet cheetah.

Josephine adopts twelve children from around the world, raising them at Les Milandes, her estate in southwestern France. She calls them her 'rainbow tribe'.

Josephine plays at New York's Carnegie Hall to a standing ovation, and is moved to tears. She begins a series of performances celebrating the fiftieth anniversary of her Paris debut.

c. 1930 — 1940s — 1950 — 1963 — 1973 — 1975

During World War Two, Josephine works for the French Resistance, hiding secret messages in her music notes as she performs around Europe. She is awarded two of France's highest military honours.

In support of the Civil Rights Movement, Josephine joins the famous March on Washington alongside her friend Martin Luther King, Jr.

Josephine dies, aged sixty-eight, at her home in Paris, France.

Josephine Baker

Frida Kahlo

PAINTER
Born – 1907, Mexico
Died – 1954, Mexico

Little Frida was fearless – she had to be. When she was small, she got very sick. The illness left Frida's leg as skinny as a rake, and she walked with a limp. Children teased her and called her names. But Frida didn't care. She played sports, rode her bicycle and learnt how to wrestle. If boys could do it, so could she!

The little girl with the limp grew up brave and strong. She dreamt she would be a doctor, and help other people who had been ill like her. Then one day, a bus Frida was riding crashed into a car. Life as she knew it changed forever. After her terrible accident, Frida had to rest in bed again. To help the hours pass, even though she was still in pain, Frida decided to paint pictures of herself using a mirror. Her mother made her a special easel she could use in bed, and her father gave her a set of soft brushes and a shiny box of paints, as bright and colourful as the ideas inside Frida's head. Slowly, one painting at a time, Frida's art got better, and so did Frida. Her dream of being a doctor was over, but now she had a new dream: she would be an artist instead!

It was time to be brave and show her pictures to someone else. She visited a famous artist, Diego Rivera, who couldn't believe his eyes – he'd never seen anything like her paintings before. Frida and Diego fell in love, and Diego encouraged Frida in her art. Frida's bold, beautiful paintings caused a great stir wherever they were shown. Even when she grew sick again, nothing could stop Frida from painting. Frida Kahlo taught the world to be courageous, to wave goodbye to bad things and say, 'Viva la vida. . .' 'Live life.'

'Feet, what do I need you for when I have wings to fly?'

Frida Kahlo

Frida Kahlo is born in the Casa Azul (Blue House) in Coyoacán, a small town outside Mexico City.

A bus crash leaves Frida with a lot of painful injuries. While she recovers, she takes up drawing and painting, mainly pictures of herself.

Frida lives in the United States, until 1934. She misses Mexico terribly.

1907 1913 1925 1928 1931 1931

Aged six, Frida becomes ill with a serious disease called polio. It leaves her with one leg skinnier than the other.

Frida sets off with her paintings under her arm to meet Diego Rivera, Mexico's most famous artist. They fall in love and marry the following year.

At an exhibition, Frida meets Georgia O'Keeffe, by then one of America's most famous artists. The two women become friends.

Five exotic pets kept by Frida
- Spider monkeys
- Mexican hairless dogs
- Parrot
- Fawn
- Eagle

Frida paints *The Two Fridas*, one of her most famous pictures. Like all her work, it shows how Frida is feeling.

At Frida's first solo exhibition in Mexico, she is so sick she turns up in an ambulance and has a bed set up for her in the gallery.

1930s | 1938 | 1939 | 1940s | 1953 | 1954

In New York City, Frida has her first solo exhibition. It's a big success.

As her health gets worse, Frida has to spend more time in bed, but she keeps painting.

Frida dies aged forty-six. As time passes, she becomes more famous, and her paintings sell for millions of dollars around the world.

Frida Kahlo

Astrid Lindgren

WRITER

Born – 1907, Sweden
Died – 2002, Sweden

Little Astrid grew up on an old farm surrounded by apple trees, in Sweden. Her childhood was very happy – so happy that she never wanted to grow up. In the summertime, Astrid and her three siblings helped in the fields and in the kitchens, where they listened to the stories and songs of the workers. Afternoons were spent roaming in fields of flowers and exploring hidden forest paths. Astrid read everything she could get her hands on. If only childhood could last forever, the little girl dreamt.

But Astrid grew up. Suddenly, she didn't want to play any more, and life seemed much more complicated. She landed her first job at a local newspaper, and when she was nineteen, became a single mum when her son Lars was born. After a while, Astrid got married and had a second child, called Karin. One night, Karin asked her mother to tell her a bedtime story about Pippi Longstocking – a funny name the little girl had just made up.

What a remarkable name, Astrid thought, I must make sure she is a remarkable girl! Astrid's Pippi was more than remarkable. She was everything a child wanted to be. She lived alone with a monkey and a horse in Villekulla, her own cottage. She was free, happy, fearless – and the strongest girl in the world!

For many years, Astrid made up stories about Pippi for Karin and her friends. When the first Pippi book was published, she became a heroine for readers all around the world. Astrid wrote many books and received many awards. A Russian astronomer even named a planet in her honour: Planet 3204 Lindgren! And today, little Astrid – the girl who never wanted to grow up – lives in our hearts through the stories of Pippi, which remind us to always try and have fun.

'A childhood without books – that would be no childhood.'

Astrid Lindgren

Astrid Anna Emilia Ericsson is born on a farm in the town of Vimmerby in the south of Sweden.

Aged thirteen, Astrid has her first story published in the *Vimmerby Times*. She is the first girl in town to get her hair cut short!

Astrid has her first child, Lars, and moves to Stockholm, where she meets Sture Lindgren. They marry and have a daughter, Karin.

1907 1910s 1921 1924 1926 1941

As a child, Astrid loves books and stories. Astrid later describes the joy of a new book as 'something almost unbearably wonderful'.

When she leaves school, Astrid is hired by the newspaper to write short reports.

Karin invents the name 'Pippi Longstocking' and asks her mother to tell her a story about her.

For Karin's tenth birthday, Astrid writes down all of the Pippi stories as a present for her. The following year, the book is published, and becomes a bestseller.

Astrid is awarded the Hans Christian Andersen medal – often called the 'Nobel Prize for Children's Literature'.

On her eightieth birthday, the Swedish prime minister gives Astrid a present – a new law to protect animals. Since the 1970s, Astrid has worked for the rights of animals, children and the environment.

1944   1946   1958   1969   1987   2002

Astrid becomes an editor at a Swedish publisher. Each morning before she goes to work, she writes stories about Pippi and other characters, like Rasmus, Ronja, Emil and Lotta.

When Pippi makes it to TV screens, Astrid works on the screenplays.

Astrid dies. Her books have sold 165 million copies and been translated into more than 100 languages.

Astrid Lindgren

Alan Turing

> **CODE-BREAKER AND FATHER OF COMPUTER SCIENCE**
>
> Born – 1912, England
>
> Died – 1954, England

Little Alan was a small, shy boy from London. But often, the quietest people achieve the most extraordinary things. At school, Alan conducted his own chemistry experiments and could solve mathematical problems in his head before his teachers taught him how. Alan loved science, and dreamt of inventing something wonderful that would change the world.

At boarding school, Alan met Christopher, a boy who shared his passion for maths and science. Alan fell deeply in love. But just as they were about to start at Cambridge University, Christopher died suddenly. Alan, who had always been lonely, felt more alone than ever – but was also determined to achieve all the things that Christopher would not be able to.

At university, he started work on a crazy idea: a machine that could calculate any sum. Alan's design was the ancestor of the computers we use today, but he didn't have the chance to build it. Half of Europe had been invaded by Germany, and Britain was at war. Alan and other brilliant minds were hired to crack the secret 'Enigma' code used by the Germans for communication. Alan quickly realised that it would take another machine – not a human mind – to beat it. His invention, a code-cracking machine called the 'Bombe', helped to win the war and saved millions of lives.

In the years after the war, Alan became the victim of terrible persecution. At that time in Britain, being gay was a crime: Alan was convicted, and lost his job. Bravely, he refused to apologise for being gay, saying he had done nothing wrong. Today, Alan is known as the hero he always was: the father of computer science, whose invention changed the world and whose courage inspires us all to stand up against prejudice.

'Sometimes it is the people no one imagines anything of who do the things that no one can imagine.'

Alan Turing

1912 — Alan Mathison Turing is born in London. He and his brother grow up away from their parents, who work overseas in India.

1926 — Aged thirteen, Alan is sent to Sherborne boarding school in Dorset. Here he meets and falls in love with Christopher Morcom – a student in the year above.

1930 — Christopher dies of tuberculosis. Alan is devastated.

1931 — Alan goes to King's College in Cambridge University to study mathematics.

1936 — At Princeton University in the US, Alan comes up with a theory for a computing device called the Turing machine – the foundation of computer science.

1939 — At the start of World War Two, Alan becomes part of the British government's code-cracking team at Bletchley Park. He invents a machine that can decipher secret messages sent by the Germans.

In 1941–42, Alan manages to decipher the more complex codes used for communication by German submarines.

Alan writes a paper that includes an idea now known as the 'Turing test' – a test to see if a computer can fool a person into believing it is human.

Alan is found dead, from cyanide poisoning, with a half-eaten apple by his side. His death is ruled a suicide. More than half a century later, Britain formally apologises for mistreating Alan and millions of other gay men.

1941 1946 1950 1952 1954 1955

After the war, Alan produces a design for the Automatic Computing Engine (ACE) – an early modern computer.

Alan is prosecuted for being gay and forced to have a medical treatment. Now with a criminal record, he loses his job at the government's code-breaking centre.

A year after Alan dies, Steve Jobs – inventor of the Apple Macintosh computer and iPhone – is born.

Alan Turing

Rosa Parks

CIVIL RIGHTS LEADER
Born – 1913, United States
Died – 2005, United States

Little Rosa grew up listening to her grandparents' stories about when their family had been enslaved. Slavery had ended, but there were still racist laws and customs where Rosa lived in Alabama. Every day, she saw the school bus taking white children to their nice, big school. The white children threw rubbish at her. White terrorists frightened and threatened her family. Rosa knew this wasn't right. She dreamt of being truly free.

When Rosa married Raymond Parks, a barber who was also an activist, he introduced her to a group that was fighting for equal rights for Black people. At the time, a terrible system called segregation kept Black people separated from white people in public places like buses and restaurants. Lots of Black people got hurt and mistreated in their city of Montgomery, and Rosa tried to help them. She became the first female leader in the local movement. The work was tiring and dangerous, but she never gave up.

One day, when Rosa was riding the city bus home, the driver demanded that she give her seat in the Black section to a white man. Rosa refused, and the driver had her taken to jail. After her arrest, she helped lead a boycott: thousands of people refused to ride the buses until the racist law changed. One year later, thanks to the work of Rosa and other leaders like her, segregation on buses was declared illegal under the US Constitution. This inspired the modern civil rights movement and made Rosa a national icon. It came at a huge cost – Rosa and her family lost their jobs and their safety, and had to leave their home. But she never stopped standing up to injustice. Today, she is remembered not just for her act of resistance on the bus, but for devoting her life to building a more just world.

'I would like to be remembered as a person who wanted to be free... so other people would be also free.'

Rosa Parks

Rosa is born in Tuskegee, Alabama.

When a white boy pushes Rosa for being Black, she pushes him back. Later, her grandmother scolds her for fighting back, and warns her she could be hurt or killed. She knows this isn't fair.

Rosa becomes the first female officer of the Montgomery NAACP, a civil rights organisation, where she will work on many important cases to help get justice, freedom and equal rights for Black citizens.

1913   1919   1923   1931   1936   1955

She lives with her grandparents near Montgomery, Alabama. A violent racist group is very active in Rosa's small town and terrorises Black families. She realises that she is not truly free.

Rosa marries Raymond Parks. He is the first activist she's ever met. He is volunteering to help free the Scottsboro Boys, a group of Black children who are sent to prison for a crime they didn't commit.

Rosa notices she's on a city bus with a cruel driver who she usually avoids. He asks everyone in the front row of the Black section to stand so a white man can sit. Rosa refuses and she is arrested.

Rosa goes to trial to fight her arrest and the Black community begins a bus boycott. That night, Rosa meets the young, unknown minister Martin Luther King, Jr., who is elected to lead the boycott.

Fleeing the South in order to find safety and work, Rosa and Raymond move to Detroit, Michigan. She continues to fight for civil rights, peace and equality.

The bus Rosa was riding when she was arrested is put on display as a national treasure in The Henry Ford museum near Detroit.

1955 1956 1957 1996 2003 2005

The US Supreme Court decides that segregation on buses is illegal. 42,000 people have taken part in the Montgomery Bus Boycott by walking, biking or carpooling for 381 days.

Rosa is known as 'the first lady of civil rights' and receives many awards, including the Presidential Medal of Freedom.

Rosa dies, leaving a legacy as a freedom fighter and pioneer of the modern-day civil rights movement.

Rosa Parks

Jesse Owens

OLYMPIC SPRINTER AND ACTIVIST

Born – 1913, United States
Died – 1980, United States

Little Jesse was the youngest of ten children. At school, he was so fast no one could catch him. But when Jesse's gym teacher asked him to join the track team, he had to say no – he had after-school jobs to help support his family and couldn't make practice. Instead, Jesse got up early and practised before sunrise. As he trained, Jesse would imagine the track was on fire, his feet barely touching the ground as he ran. He was determined to follow his dream of being an athlete.

At university, Jesse had great success on the track, despite not being able to eat, wash or sleep in the same places as his white fellow students. At one championship, he set three world records and tied a fourth… in 45 minutes! It was one of the most celebrated moments in the history of sport.

Still dreaming of being the best athlete in the world, Jesse represented America at the 1936 Olympics in Berlin, Germany. At the time, Germany was ruled by a terrible man called Adolf Hitler, who didn't think Black athletes should be allowed to compete. Jesse won four gold medals and became the fastest man in history, stealing the spotlight from Hitler's hateful government.

Back in America, Jesse was still not treated equally. He had to use the servants' entrance at his own celebration dinner for his Olympic win; the main door was only for white people. Finally, thirty years after his great Olympic victory, he was awarded the Presidential Medal of Freedom, the highest civilian award for an American. Jesse struggled against injustice and racism much of his life, but at each Olympics, Jesse is remembered: that little boy, running on the strength of his feet and the courage of his lungs, who fought the wind and dreamt of a better world.

'Find the good. It's all around you. Find it, showcase it and you'll start believing in it.'

Jesse Owens

1918 — James Cleveland Owens is born, the last of ten children, to cotton farmers in Alabama.

1928 — Encouraged by Riley, Jesse equals the world record in the 100-yard dash, running it in 9.4 seconds at the National High School Championship in Chicago.

1934 — Nicknamed the 'Buckeye Bullet', Jesse is the first African-American to be team captain, but still faces much discrimination. He must wait for his white teammates to finish showering before he can wash himself.

1932 — To support his family, Jesse works after school in a shoe repair shop as well as loading freight cars and delivering groceries. It means he can't practise with his track team, but the coach, Charles Riley, allows him to train before school instead.

1935 — At university, Jesse is a star on the track. As an African-American, he is not eligible for a scholarship, so has to work part-time jobs to pay his way through university.

1935 — Known as one of the most impressive moments in sports history, Jesse wins three athletics world records and ties a fourth, all in the space of about 45 minutes. His record for the long jump holds for the next twenty-five years.

At the Olympic Games in Germany, leader Adolf Hitler criticises America for allowing Black athletes to compete. Jesse wins four gold medals, challenging people around the world to stand up to racism.

After the Olympics, Jesse has a hard time finding work. For the next twenty years, he works in a string of jobs, including at a petrol station and in a jazz band.

After retiring, Jesse is awarded the Presidential Medal of Freedom by the American President, Gerald Ford. A few years later, he is given the Living Legend Award by President Jimmy Carter.

1936   1936   1937   1955   1976   1980

Despite his Olympic success, Jesse is made to enter by the servants' entrance at a dinner held in his honour in New York City. President Roosevelt fails to welcome him to the White House or send him a telegram of congratulations.

Jesse is made a Goodwill Ambassador for the US government. He tours the world, advancing the Olympic cause and attending sporting events.

Jesse dies in Tuscon, Arizona. That same year, a newly discovered asteroid – 6758 Jesseowens – is named after him.

Jesse Owens

Ella Fitzgerald

JAZZ SINGER

Born – 1917, United States
Died – 1996, United States

Little Ella grew up with her family in Yonkers, New York. She had a beautiful voice, but her first dream was to dance. She would take the train to Harlem to see her favourite performers and entertain her friends with her singing. But one day, tragedy struck. Her mother died suddenly in a car accident. Ella was heartbroken. She went to live with her aunt, but didn't like her new life. She started skipping school and got into trouble. After being treated very badly at her new school, she ran away and had to make a living singing and dancing on street corners in Harlem.

One night, Ella entered a competition to dance at one of New York's most famous theatres. At the last minute, she chose to sing instead. She dazzled the crowd with her sweet, tuneful voice and won first prize! Afterwards, Ella was so excited she couldn't sleep. Now she dreamt of singing, accompanied by her very own orchestra.

Ella's talent was soon noticed by big band leader, Chick Webb, who offered her the chance to travel and sing at jazz clubs around the country. Ella never sang a song the same way twice. She turned somersaults with her voice and could imitate every instrument in the band.

When Ella decided it was time to go solo, all the jazz greats wanted to perform with her. Ella mastered show tunes, pop, opera and blues, taking her music to new places. She became famous around the world, and made sure all people could watch her shows together and not be segregated by the colour of their skin. When she retired, little Ella – who imagined stepping off the street corner and singing with her own orchestra, and who dared to speak up for others – was truly the First Lady of Song, an inspiration to every little girl dreaming of a bigger stage.

'It isn't where you came from; it's where you're going that counts.'

Ella Fitzgerald

1917 — Ella Jane Fitzgerald is born in Newport News, Virginia, before moving with her family to Yonkers, near New York City.

c. 1930 — Taking the train to Harlem to see her favourite musicians and performers, Ella gets to see many of the jazz greats of the time.

1932 — Ella's mother dies in a car accident. Soon after, Ella is sent to live with her aunt, before being sent away to reform school.

1933 — During the Great Depression in America, Ella runs away from school, and has to dance on the streets of Harlem to make enough money to survive.

1934 — Aged seventeen, Ella enters the Apollo Theatre's amateur talent competition. Ella is planning to dance, but changes her mind and decides to sing instead. She wins over the crowd and is awarded first prize.

1935 — Ella is spotted by band leader Chick Webb and they record many songs together, touring American jazz clubs. After a few years, they have their first hit with a song called 'A-Tisket, A-Tasket'.

When Chick Webb dies, Ella takes over the band for the next three years. She records more than 100 songs during this time.

Ella wins two awards at the first Grammy Awards. She goes on to win thirteen Grammys over the course of her career.

Ella gives her final concert at Carnegie Hall in New York City, age seventy-four.

1939 1942 1956 1968 1991 1996

After leaving Chick's band and going solo, Ella begins scatting, with all kinds of new vocalisations that hadn't been heard before. That same year, she makes her film debut.

Not long after Martin Luther King, Jr's assassination, Ella records the song 'He had a dream' in honour of him.

Ella dies. In the course of her fifty-year career, she recorded over 2,000 songs, sang with all the jazz greats and was awarded the Presidential Medal of Freedom.

Ella Fitzgerald

David Attenborough

Maya Angelou

Martin Luther King, Jr.

Audrey Hepburn

Anne Frank

Corazon Aquino

Jane Goodall

Rudolf Nureyev

Wilma Rudolph

John Lennon

1920 - 1940

David Attenborough

BROADCASTER AND NATURALIST

Born – 1926, England

Little David loved nature and animals from a young age. Ants, birds, chameleons... he was fascinated by all of the species he read about in books, and wished he could meet them in real life. He often went on long bicycle rides to the countryside to collect fossils and plants. It wasn't long before David knew that he wanted to be a naturalist. He dreamt that he could share his love for nature with the rest of the world and show others its wonder.

After studying zoology and geology at university, David joined the BBC and began to make television shows. One of his first programmes featured zoo animals he would bring into the studio. But David dreamt of seeing animals in their natural habitats and homes, wherever that might be. He began travelling all over the world, showing viewers at home the amazing lives of faraway plants and animals. He met turtles on the Galapagos Islands and gorillas in the African jungle. When he visited Antarctica, he was introduced to all the members of a penguin family. One of his programmes, *Wildlife on One*, became the most popular in British history.

David continued to make nature documentaries, many of them groundbreaking for their time and watched by millions. For his services, he was knighted by the Queen – not once, but twice! Many plants and animals have been named after David: a rare butterfly, a snail, a prehistoric lion, a spider... and even a carnivorous plant. Little David grew up to be a much-loved star of the screen, who showed us the enormous beauty in the world. Now in his nineties, David continues to teach us how to protect and nurture our planet, so that we can create a better, cleaner, less-polluted Earth, filled with healthy, happy animals of all kinds, shapes and sizes.

'We can now destroy or we can cherish — the choice is ours.'

David Attenborough

David Attenborough is born in London, England, before his family moves north to Leicester.

David wins a scholarship to study natural sciences at Cambridge University.

David launches and presents *Zoo Quest*, a TV programme that visits animals in zoos or in the wild.

1926 c.1936 1945 1952 1954 1969

Not long after attending a lecture by famous naturalist Grey Owl, David is inspired to become a naturalist.

After training, David begins work at the BBC, behind the scenes as a TV producer.

As BBC's Director of Television Programming, David commissions iconic shows such as *Match of the Day*, *Monty Python's Flying Circus* and *The Ascent of Man*.

David launches *Life on Earth*, travelling the world and using cutting-edge filming to view animals in their environment, in ways they'd never been seen before.

Planet Earth airs on TV, with David narrating. It is the biggest wildlife documentary ever made.

David meets climate activist Greta Thunberg via video call, to discuss their hopes for the planet's future.

1979   1985   2006   2016   2019   2021

David is knighted by Queen Elizabeth II for his services to broadcasting and conservation. He is knighted again in 2020.

David, the oldest person to have visited the North Pole, has a British polar research ship named after him.

Now in his nineties, David has written, narrated or presented over 100 documentaries. He continues to talk and write about our pressing need to protect our environment.

David Attenborough

Maya Angelou

WRITER, SPEAKER AND ACTIVIST

Born – 1928, United States
Died – 2014, United States

Little Maya was born in St Louis. When Maya was very young, she and her brother went to live with their grandmother in a small Southern town. There, Maya had to deal with racist laws and customs, and a scary group called the Ku Klux Klan who terrorised Black people. Maya, who was shy by nature, was often terrified of doing or saying something wrong. She dreamed of what it would feel like to be comfortable in her own skin.

When Maya was eight years old, she was the victim of abuse. She was so frightened by the experience that she stopped speaking in public for five years. During this time, Maya discovered the joys of books, and found her voice again by reading aloud the wonderful stories and poems of great writers.

Maya was a brilliant student, but no one believed in her. Racism and sexism against Black women meant she would have to make her own path in life. So, she did. She became a singer, a dancer, a streetcar conductor, a cook, an actor, a director, a journalist, a playwright, a composer and a screenwriter. Her work took her all around the world. She joined the campaign for civil rights, becoming friends and colleagues with Malcolm X and Martin Luther King, Jr.

Maya put her incredible life story into writing, with the book *I Know Why the Caged Bird Sings*. It was an immediate success. Her story was her own, but it was also the story of so many people who had gone unheard for too long. She went on to write many more books, and became a thrilling speaker and professor. She never stopped finding and sharing wisdom, joy and hope. Once a little girl who was afraid to talk, Maya is remembered all over the world for her remarkable voice.

'We may encounter many defeats, but we must not be defeated.'

Maya Angelou

Maya is born. Three years later, she and her brother travel alone by train to Stamps, Arkansas.

'Maya Angelou' is a stage name that Maya choses while working as a calypso dancer.

Maya moves to Egypt and begins working as a journalist. She later lives in Ghana for several years.

1928 1944 1955 1960 1961 1968

Maya becomes San Francisco's first Black and first female streetcar conductor.

Maya organizes 'Cabaret for Freedom' to raise money for Martin Luther King, Jr.'s civil rights organisation.

Maya begins writing a book about her incredible life.

I Know Why the Caged Bird Sings is nominated for a National Book Award and is a bestseller.

Maya becomes a professor of American Studies at Wake Forest University.

Maya is awarded the Presidential Medal of Freedom by US President Barack Obama.

1970   1973   1982   1993   2010   2014

Maya receives a Tony Award nomination for acting in the Broadway play *Look Away*.

Maya recites her poem 'On the Pulse of Morning' at US President Bill Clinton's inauguration. She is the first Black and first female inaugural poet.

Maya dies, leaving behind a legacy of inspiration, courage and hope.

Martin Luther King, Jr.

CIVIL RIGHTS LEADER

Born – 1929, United States
Died – 1968, United States

Growing up in a family of pastors, little Martin quickly learnt to tell the difference between right and wrong. He was born into a country that was deeply divided by segregation – a law that kept Black and white people separate in public places like restaurants, buses and schools. One day, a friend invited him over to play, but Martin was asked to leave because he was African-American. Martin was shocked. He promised himself that he would always fight injustice. His dream was a world where all people were equal.

As he grew older, Martin realised that the best way to change people's hearts and minds was through words – the most powerful thing of all. He became a pastor of a church in Montgomery, Alabama, and gave passionate sermons that inspired a new sense of hope. When Rosa Parks was arrested for refusing to give up her seat to a white man on a bus, Martin joined with people in his community to boycott the city's buses until the law was changed – and the tactic worked!

This was the first major civil rights action in America... but not the last. Martin encouraged people all over the country to stand up for their rights, using peaceful protest. They were often attacked, and Martin was arrested twenty-nine times, but he never fought back with force. Martin knew that hate can't stop hate; only love can. During a protest march on Washington, he gave a life-changing speech that included four simple yet powerful words: 'I have a dream'.

Martin's words of hope, peace and justice called a nation to change its laws and make them equal for everyone. And little Martin's dream, of a world where we are judged by our character, not by the colour of our skin, continues to inspire the world to action today.

'The time is always right to do what is right.'

Martin Luther King, Jr.

Martin Luther King, Jr. is born 'Michael' in Atlanta, Georgia, but later changes his name to Martin.

Super-smart Martin starts university aged fifteen.

Martin joins with his community to bring about the first African-American non-violent demonstration, known as the 'bus boycott'. He is arrested for the first time.

1929 1935 1944 1954 1955 1957

When he is six, Martin is asked to leave a friend's house because he is Black. Later, he and his friend are sent to separate, segregated schools.

Martin moves to Alabama, and becomes the pastor of a church in Montgomery.

Martin helps to set up the Southern Christian Leadership Conference (SCLC), which leads many non-violent protests against segregation.

Martin visits the birthplace of the Indian civil rights leader, Mahatma Gandhi. The trip strengthens Martin's belief in non-violence.

At the March on Washington, Martin delivers his famous 'I have a dream' speech to a crowd of 250,000 people.

Martin marches to Montgomery, Alabama, in support of African-American voting rights. The Voting Rights Act becomes law the following year.

1959   1960   1963   1964   1965   1968

Martin joins African American college students in a sit-in at a segregated lunch counter. He is arrested, but is later released.

The Civil Rights Act makes segregation in public places, like schools and buses, illegal. Later that year, Martin becomes the youngest person to win the Nobel Peace Prize.

Martin is shot and killed. Today, he is honoured in the US by a public holiday on the third Monday in January – Martin Luther King Day.

Audrey Hepburn

> **ACTOR, DANCER AND HUMANITARIAN**
>
> Born – 1929, Belgium
> Died – 1993, Switzerland

Little Audrey lived in a town called Arnhem, in the Netherlands. She dreamt of what she would do when she grew up... Would she become a ballerina – or maybe an actress? But one day, on her way to ballet class, Audrey saw soldiers on the streets. World War Two had broken out. She watched many Jewish families being put on trains and sent to concentration camps – including children just like her. It was a hard time for Audrey and all the other children. There was very little food and they were often hungry. Opposed to the German occupation of her country, Audrey, along with many other young people, helped the Dutch Resistance by delivering messages.

After the war, Audrey moved to London to study dance. Her teacher said she was too weak from the war to become a ballerina. But Audrey didn't give up. She decided she would act and dance in musicals instead! Before long, she was on stage in London and New York, and starring in films people love to this day. Every role she played was different – one day she was a nun, and the next... a princess! Audrey won award after award. Yet she never forgot that there were children in the world who were hungry, just like she had been.

Audrey became an official ambassador for UNICEF, a charity that visited children all over the world, helping to raise money to provide them with water, food and medicine. Wherever she went, Audrey tried to make every child happy. Because she remembered how she had felt when she was a child in need, Audrey spent the rest of her life helping people across the globe. And that made her happier than acting or dancing ever had.

'Dance as though no one is watching.
Sing as though no one can hear you.'

Audrey Hepburn

Audrey Kathleen Ruston is born in Brussels, Belgium. Her mother, Ella van Heemstra, was a Dutch baroness and her father, Joseph Ruston, was British.

World War Two breaks out and the people of the Netherlands suffer famine, bombings and German occupation. In desperation, Audrey's hungry family grind tulip bulbs to make flour.

Audrey lands her first role in a London musical, *High Button Shoes*, and goes on to play more small parts on the British stage.

1929 1932 1939 1945 1948 1951

Audrey and her mother move to Arnhem, a small town in the Netherlands, and Audrey starts ballet lessons.

After the war, Audrey trains to be a ballerina in London, but malnutrition has weakened her – she pursues acting instead.

To great acclaim, Audrey stars in the Broadway production of *Gigi*, based on the book by French writer Colette.

106

Audrey stars in *Roman Holiday*, the first of many Hollywood films, winning an Oscar for best actress.

Audrey meets Otto Frank, the father of Jewish diarist Anne Frank, who died in a concentration camp in 1945. Anne's story is felt deeply by Audrey, who lived only 100 km from Anne and was the same age.

Audrey travels to Ethiopia to show the world the desperate situation there caused by famine and war. UNICEF honours Audrey for her humanitarian work.

1953 1954 1957 1988 1988 1993

Now a famous film star, Audrey acts in *Sabrina*, *Funny Face*, *Breakfast at Tiffany's* and *My Fair Lady*, while also performing on stage.

Audrey never forgets the experience of going without food as a child. After retiring, she becomes a UNICEF Goodwill Ambassador.

Audrey dies at her home in Switzerland, aged sixty-four.

Audrey Hepburn

Anne Frank

DIARIST

Born – 1929, Germany
Died – 1945, Germany

Little Anne was a Jewish girl who lived happily with her family in Germany. When she was four, a man named Adolf Hitler became leader of the country. He and his Nazi government hated Jewish people, and Anne's family was forced to move to the Netherlands for safety. Here, she learnt how to speak Dutch and made lots of friends. But when World War Two broke out, the Nazis invaded half of Europe – including the Netherlands. Anne and all the other Jewish children were forced to go to separate schools and wear a star on their chest.

Scared of being arrested, Anne's family decided to go into hiding. They moved to a secret annex where they lived for two years, sharing the cramped space with another Jewish family. Anne recorded her strange, difficult new life in a diary she had been given for her thirteenth birthday. She wrote about family arguments, her favourite film stars, the fear of being discovered, her hopes of being a writer – and her dream of a better world, with no hate or war. 'I still believe, in spite of everything, that people are really good at heart', she wrote.

One day, Anne stopped writing. Nazi soldiers had found their hideaway. The family was pushed onto a train full of people on its way to a concentration camp. It took three long days for them to arrive at the worst place on Earth. Anne's father, Otto, was the only member of the family to survive the war. When he later found his young daughter's diary, Otto wept. He decided to publish it and share Anne's story, just as she would have wanted. Since then, millions of people have read and cried over *The Diary of Anne Frank*, the story of the little girl who dreamt of a better world.

'You can always give something, even if it is only kindness.'

Anne Frank

Annelies Frank (known as 'Anne') is born in Frankfurt, in Germany. She grows up with her parents, Otto and Edith, and an older sister, Margot.

Like many Jewish people, Anna's family decide to leave Germany. They move to the Netherlands when Anne is four years old.

World War Two breaks out. The following year, Germany invades the Netherlands and the Nazis introduce strict laws: Jewish people cannot own businesses, go to the cinema, visit certain shops, or attend the same schools as non-Jews. They are forced to wear stars on their clothing.

1929 1933 1934 1934 1939 1940

Adolf Hitler of the Nazi Party becomes leader of Germany. He blames Jewish people for Germany's poverty and unemployment.

Anne starts school in Amsterdam, and goes on to become a star pupil. She spends her spare time playing with friends and reading.

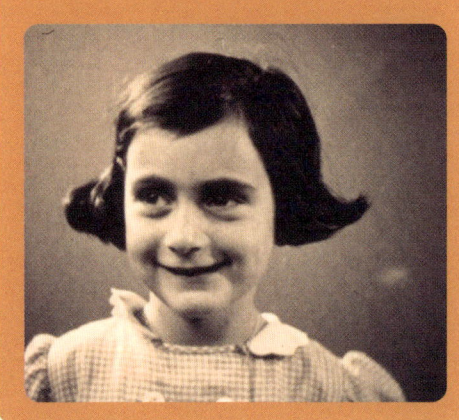

Elsewhere in Europe, American-born performer Josephine Baker fights Nazi Germany by working as a spy for the French Resistance.

On her thirteenth birthday, on June 12th, Anne is given a diary, which she names Kitty.

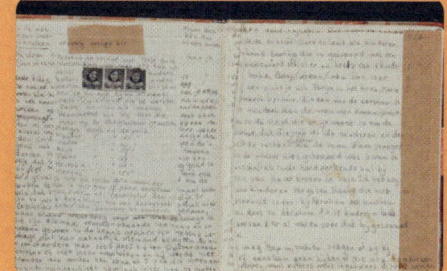

For two years, eight people share the tiny space. Everyone has to stay very quiet, speaking in whispers and walking barefoot. Anne finds it very difficult.

In August, German police break into the annex and arrest Anne's family, who are all sent to concentration camps. In these camps, millions of people (most of them Jewish) are killed – some are murdered, while others are forced to work and die from starvation or disease. Back in Amsterdam, one of Otto's helpers discovers Anne's diary and keeps it safe.

1942 1942 1942 1944 1944 1945

On July 6th, Anne's family go into hiding in a secret annex, tucked behind a bookshelf at Otto's work. They are joined by another family, Peter Van Pels and his parents, and a dentist called Fritz Pfeffer. Four of Otto's old employees help bring the family supplies.

Anne writes in her diary that she wants to be a journalist when she grows up, so she can be useful, and go on living after her death.

Fifteen-year-old Anne dies of a disease called typhus in the camp. Her mother and sister also die. In 1947, Otto publishes Anne's diary, which goes on to sell millions of copies around the world. Anne lives on through her words and in all those who read her story.

Anne Frank

Corazon Aquino

POLITICAL LEADER

Born – 1933, Philippines
Died – 2009, Philippines

Little Cory was born in the Philippines, a beautiful country with thousands of islands. As a child, she was shy and serious, but always took a step forward when it was needed – even when it was something scary, like giving a speech to the entire school! The brave little girl grew up to become a young woman with a great sense of justice. She decided to become a lawyer: that way, she dreamt, she could play her part in making her country a better, fairer place.

At university, Cory fell in love with a young man named Ninoy, who was as honest and fair-minded as she was. With Cory by his side, Ninoy quickly became one of the country's brightest young leaders, challenging the rule of the corrupt, dishonest president, Ferdinand Marcos. One day, Marcos declared a law that stripped citizens of their democratic rights. Ninoy was arrested and flung into prison. For seven long years, Cory became her husband's voice, making speeches and keeping the dream of democracy alive.

Finally, Ninoy was released, and the family moved to America, where they spent the happiest three years of their lives. Sadly, it did not last. Ninoy returned to the Philippines and was killed. Cory was now all alone... and yet, she wasn't! Millions of people threw aside their fear and stayed by her side at Ninoy's funeral.

Cory became a symbol of hope for her people. Even though she had no experience, she decided to run for president. When Marcos faked the election results, claiming he had won, people took to the streets to proclaim Cory the rightful president. It was a victory for democracy. With the whole world watching, Cory became the first female president of the Philippines – the courageous, honest woman who wrote herself into the history books, and the hearts of her people.

'I just do whatever it is that I believe I should do, regardless of the risks to my life.'

Corazon Aquino

Maria Corazon Sumulong Cojuangco (called 'Cory') is born near Manila in the Philippines.	Thirteen-year-old Corazon is sent to high school in America. She stays on to complete a degree in mathematics and French. 	Corazon and Ninoy marry, and Corazon drops out of her law course. The couple have five children together – one son and four daughters. 

1933 · **1930s** · **1946** · **1953** · **1954** · **1956**

As a young girl, Corazon is shy and hardworking. Her family is very wealthy, but she is not spoilt. 	Corazon returns to the Philippines to study law, and falls in love with a young journalist, Benigno Aquino, Jr. – 'Ninoy' to his friends. 	When Ninoy decides to become a politician, Cory sells her most beloved heirlooms to support him. Ninoy becomes a tough critic of the corrupt president, Ferdinand Marcos. 

1972

The president declares a law that gives him sole control of the country. Ninoy is arrested, and spends seven years, seven months in prison. During this time, Corazon passes her husband's notes to the press.

1980

When Ninoy is released, the family moves to the United States for three years. Corazon is very happy there.

1983

Ninoy returns to the Philippines and is killed as soon as he sets foot off the plane. The grieving Corazon wins the love and support of the Filipino people.

1986

Corazon challenges Marcos at the election, and becomes the first female president of the Philippines. The country celebrates!

1986

TIME magazine names Corazon 'Woman of the Year'.

2009

Corazon dies. A few months later, her son is elected president of the Philippines.

Corazon Aquino

Jane Goodall

PRIMATOLOGIST AND CONSERVATIONIST

Born – 1934, England

When Jane was a little girl, her father gave her a stuffed chimpanzee called Jubilee. Wherever Jane went, Jubilee came too. The cuddly toy sparked a love of animals in Jane that never left her. She dreamt of living in the jungle in Africa with wild chimpanzees, just like the heroes of her bedtime stories.

Jane couldn't afford to go to university to study animals, but she didn't give up her dream. She saved every penny she had until she could buy a boat ticket to Kenya, in Africa. There, she met a well-known scientist called Louis Leakey, who was looking for a researcher to study chimpanzees in the wild. So, equipped with little more than binoculars and a notebook, Jane took another journey to the shores of Gombe, in Tanzania.

Here, Jane waited patiently, day after day, and finally the chimpanzees accepted her. Instead of numbering each chimpanzee, as other scientists did, Jane gave them names that suited their personalities or appearance. She noticed that some chimps were kind, quiet and generous, while others were bullies. Then, Jane made another incredible discovery: chimpanzees could make their own tools – something only humans were thought to do. The news rocked the scientific world! It seemed that humans and chimps were not so different, after all.

Jane's talent was quickly recognised by Cambridge University, where she studied for her doctorate in animal behaviour. She became a world-leading expert on chimpanzees, and later – when she realised that jungles were starting to disappear across Africa – she became a passionate conservationist, too. And today, the little girl who loved animals challenges us all to be kind to nature, because every single one of us can make a difference to the future of our planet.

'Every individual matters. Every individual has a role to play. Every individual makes a difference.'

Jane Goodall

1934 — Valerie Jane Morris-Goodall ('Jane') is born in London.

1957 — After working for five years, Jane saves enough money to go to Kenya, in Africa. Here, she meets famous anthropologist and palaeontologist Dr Louis Leakey, who hires her to research chimps in the wild.

1961 — Jane's three major discoveries
- Chimps use tools, just like humans
- Chimps have personalities and show emotions
- Chimps are not vegetarian, but eat meat

1930s — Jane is given a stuffed chimpanzee toy. She grows up with a love of animals. Her pets include a dog, a pony and a tortoise.

1960 — Jane heads to Gombe Stream Chimpanzee Reserve in Tanzania, where she is accepted into a chimpanzee society. She lives with them for twenty-two months.

1962 — Jane studies for a doctorate at Cambridge University.

Back in Tanzania, Jane sets up the Gombe Stream Research Centre.

Broadcaster David Attenborough launches *Life On Earth*, his landmark nature documentary TV series. David and Jane share a passion for conservation, and later become friends.

Jane becomes a United Nations Messenger of Peace – one of many accolades and awards she is given during her career.

1965 1977 1979 1986 2002 2021

Jane establishes the Jane Goodall Foundation. It works with local communities to protect chimpanzees and their habitat.

Jane shifts her focus to conservation. In 1991, she sets up Roots & Shoots, which encourages young people to protect wildlife and the environment.

Jane continues to dedicate her life to conservation and education. She travels the world giving speeches, accompanied by Mr H – her stuffed monkey sidekick.

Jane Goodall

Rudolf Nureyev

> **DANCER**
>
> Born – 1938, Russia
> Died – 1993, France

Born on a train, speeding across Siberia, little Rudolf was in constant motion from the moment he entered the world. He grew up in a tiny wooden house in the north of Russia, where winters were fierce and life was hard. One day, Rudolf's mother scraped together just enough money to take her children to the ballet. It was a moment that would change Rudolf's life. As he watched the dancers whirl across the stage, the little boy dreamt that one day, he would join them.

Rudolf asked for lessons, but his father disapproved. He thought ballet was just for girls. When Rudolf eventually found his way to a professional ballet school, he discovered he was not as good as the other dancers. But this only made him even more determined – he would simply have to work harder, and harder, until he was the very best! Soon, he became one of the leading figures at the famous Kirov Ballet.

Rudolf's ballet company travelled to Paris. The Parisienne audiences adored the passionate Russian dancer, and Rudolf adored Paris, too. The movies, the fancy shops, the parties... it was so different from Russia, where many things were not allowed. On the day of his departure, Rudolf ran away from the Russian secret agents who were watching him and refused to get on the plane. 'I want to stay and be free,' he declared.

Now, nothing and no one could hold Rudolf back. He was free to dance and live and love as he wanted. Over the next thirty years, he danced almost every role with every company in the world, and made his dreams come true. His electrifying performances and star power showed the world that there are no 'things for girls' nor 'things for boys', only things that you love doing with your whole heart.

'You live as long as you dance.'

Rudolf Nureyev

Rudolf is born in Russia, aboard the Trans-Siberian Express train.

On New Year's Eve, Rudolf's mother manages to buy a single ticket to the ballet, and sneaks her children in. Rudolf is instantly captivated.

At seventeen, Rudolf joins the prestigious Kirov Ballet School in Leningrad – much later than other dancers. He works very hard to catch up.

1938 **1940s** **1945** **1949** **1955** **1958**

Rudolf grows up in poverty. When he is five, his mother has to carry him to school on her back through the snow because he doesn't have any shoes.

Aged eleven, Rudolf starts ballet lessons.

Rudolf is accepted into the Kirov Ballet, and immediately starts making a reputation for himself.

On a trip to Paris, Rudolf refuses to return to Russia and decides to stay in the West.

In the 1960s and 1970s, Rudolf dances for major ballet companies around the world. He starts to choreograph his own ballets, too.

Finally, Rudolf is allowed to return to Russia – for the first time in over twenty-five years.

1961 1962 1960s 1983 1987 1993

Rudolf first dances with the famous ballerina Margot Fonteyn. They develop a famous partnership. Audiences love them like rock stars.

Rudolf becomes dance director at the Paris Opéra Ballet.

Rudolf dies, near Paris. He is remembered as one of the greatest dancers of all time.

Rudolf Nureyev

Wilma Rudolph

> **OLYMPIC SPRINTER, TEACHER AND ACTIVIST**
>
> Born – 1940, United States
> Died – 1994, United States

Little Wilma was the tiniest baby in Tennessee, or so her nineteen siblings thought. When Wilma was four, she got an illness called polio. The doctors said she wouldn't walk again, but her mother told Wilma that she would – and Wilma believed her. Wilma dreamt that, one day, she would run even faster than a gazelle.

Twice a week, Wilma and her mum visited the hospital, and back home, her siblings took turns rubbing her leg like the nurses at the hospital, four times a day. Her family's care and attention worked: by age nine, Wilma could walk without her leg brace. Now there was no turning back.

Just like her older sister, Wilma began playing basketball. She scored 803 points in less than a year for her high school basketball team, leading them to the state championship. In sprints, she ran so fast that few could catch her. Soon, an athletics coach at the nearby university noticed her speed. Impressed, he asked her to go on a training programme for young athletes.

At the age of sixteen, Wilma became the youngest US team member at the Olympic Games in Australia, where she sprinted to a bronze medal. Four years later, at the Olympics in Rome, she truly earned her nickname, 'Gazelle', and became the first woman to win three gold medals. When the state governor wanted to give her a welcome parade on her return, she insisted that he allow people of all colours to join the celebration or she wouldn't go.

After retiring, Wilma taught other athletes and young people, travelling the world to help others and promote equal rights. By refusing to give up, little Wilma, who dreamt of not just walking but running, who fought to be treated the same as anyone else, became the fastest woman in the world and an inspiration to all.

'Never underestimate the power of dreams and the influence of the human spirit.'

Wilma Rudolph

Wilma is born in Saint Bethlehem, Tennessee, the twentieth of twenty-two children from her father's two marriages. She is born premature, and weighs just 2 kg.

For two years, twice a week, Wilma and her mother take the bus 80 km to a hospital that is willing to treat her leg – the local hospital is for white people only.

Fourteen-year-old Wilma is asked to join a summer training programme for athletes at Tennessee State University. She begins to compete regularly at amateur track events, winning them all.

1940   1944   1946   1949   1954   1956

When she is four, having already had pneumonia and scarlet fever, Wilma contracts polio. Her left leg loses strength and becomes twisted.

Wilma is finally able to take her brace off and starts to wear a special shoe. After removing the shoe, she can run faster than any boy in her neighbourhood.

After qualifying to compete in the 200-metre event, Wilma becomes the youngest member of the US Olympic team. She wins a bronze medal in Australia.

126

Now a student at Tennessee State University, Wilma sets a world record during her trials for the 200-metre dash. At the Olympics in Rome, Italy, she becomes the first American woman to win three gold medals.

Wilma retires, explaining that she wants to leave the sport while still at her best – just like her hero, Olympic sprinter Jesse Owens.

Wilma's autobiography is published, paving the way over the next few years for a film and over twenty books, mostly aimed at schoolchildren, which feature the inspirational story of her life.

1960 **1960** **1962** **1963** **1977** **1994**

On her return to her hometown of Clarksville, Wilma insists that the celebratory banquet and parade held in her honour not be segregated. It becomes the first fully integrated event in the city's history.

Wilma graduates from Tennessee State University with a degree in Education. She becomes a Goodwill Ambassador for the US government, travelling to different countries to attend sporting events and visit schools before returning to teach in her former school.

Wilma dies aged fifty-four. Her legacy of helping others fight for equality, while teaching young people to reach for their dreams, carries on.

Wilma Rudolph

John Lennon

> **SINGER-SONGWRITER AND PEACE ACTIVIST**
>
> Born – 1940, England
> Died – 1980, United States

Little John was born in the city of Liverpool towards the end of World War Two. At night, he could hear bombs falling. Life wasn't easy – his father was away at sea and his mother found it hard. Eventually, he went to live with his aunt and uncle, though his mother would visit often. John loved drawing, often doodling rather than listening to the teachers. But when his mother bought him a guitar, John knew what he wanted to do with his life. He dreamt of being like Elvis Presley and other American blues and rock-and-roll musicians.

John formed a band with some schoolmates and soon, a friend called Paul joined them. Paul was more into pop, while John was a rock-and-roll rebel. They became 'The Beatles', performing at a Liverpool club called The Cavern, where everyone laughed at John's silly jokes and antics. Soon after, the band's first song was released, and The Beatles quickly became the biggest band on the planet.

John, Paul, Ringo and George played all over the world and even for the Queen. Their fans screamed so loud when they went on stage that John couldn't even hear himself sing!

One day, John met a Japanese artist called Yoko at a London gallery, where she gave John a card that said 'Breathe'. They were together from that day on. After making twelve albums with The Beatles, full of some of the greatest songs in the history of music, John left the band, but he carried on making music. In his most famous song, 'Imagine', John played the piano and sang about his dreams for a world without war. On their honeymoon, Yoko and John set up a 'peace camp' in their hotel room and became an inspiration for the anti-war movement. Little John is still remembered as one of the world's greatest songwriters, and one who keeps inspiring us to imagine a world where all people live in peace.

'You don't need anybody to tell you who you are or what you are. You are what you are!'

John Lennon

1940 — John Winston Lennon is born in Liverpool, towards the end of World War Two.

1944 — John moves in with his eldest aunt, Mimi, when he is four. They are often visited by John's mum, Julia, who shows him how to play the banjo and eventually buys him his first guitar.

1948 — John spends the rest of his childhood with his Aunt Mimi and Uncle George, who have no children of their own. He loves to draw comics and spends time with his cousins, often going to Blackpool to watch shows.

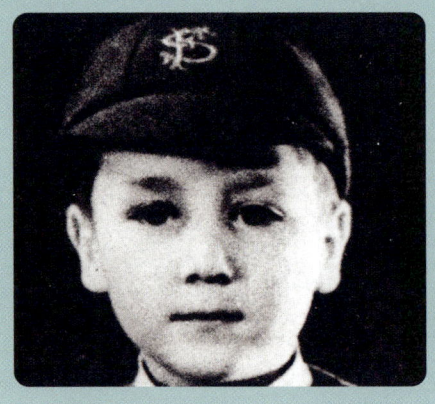

1956 — John forms his first band, The Quarrymen. He plays at a church garden fête and meets Paul McCartney, asking him to join the band.

1960 — The band becomes The Beatles and plays a forty-eight-night residency (series of concerts) in Hamburg, West Germany.

1962 — Brian Epstein becomes the manager of The Beatles, despite having never managed musicians or artists before. He focuses on their look, changing John's rockabilly style, and insists they wear suits.

The Beatles record their first album *Please Please Me* in under ten hours.

John marries Yoko Ono. They celebrate their honeymoon by staging a 'bed-in for peace' for two weeks in a hotel room. That same year, John writes 'Give Peace A Chance', and it becomes an anti-war anthem.

In his last live performance, John plays on stage at Madison Square Garden in New York with his good friend Elton John.

1963   1964   1969   1970   1974   1980

Beatlemania takes hold – the band plays for the Queen and sets off on a US tour. Over the next few years, the Beatles become the most famous band in the world and their songs change music forever.

John officially leaves The Beatles, though he has been writing solo material and creating music with Yoko Ono for some years.

The world is shocked when John is shot by an ill fan, and dies. He is forty years old.

John Lennon

Pelé

Bruce Lee

Vivienne Westwood

Bob Dylan

Stephen Hawking

Muhammad Ali

Aretha Franklin

Billie Jean King

Dolly Parton

David Bowie

1940 - 1947

Pelé

FOOTBALLER AND ACTIVIST

Born – 1940, Brazil

Little Edson, Pelé to his friends, began playing football on the streets of Brazil. Using a ball made from a sock stuffed with newspapers and tightened with string, Pelé dreamt of playing for a real team, with a real ball. One day, he came home and found his father in tears. Brazil had lost the football World Cup final! Pelé made a promise to him: one day, he would win that championship for his father.

After playing indoor football, a coach convinced Pelé's mother to let him quit the shoe factory where he worked. He wanted him to move to the city of Santos and try out for their team. When club managers saw this fifteen-year-old boy dancing samba with a ball, they couldn't believe their eyes. He controlled the ball like no other, performing spectacular tricks with both feet, and scoring goals with all parts of his body... even his bum! In his debut match, Pelé scored his first official goal, and soon he was the season's top scorer. Pelé was sixteen when he played for Brazil in the World Cup in Sweden. Fans everywhere celebrated his goals, as Pelé played his 'jogo bonito', or 'beautiful game'. Brazil won the World Cup for the first time ever and the whole country cried with joy.

Pelé was named football's 'O Rei', or 'The King'. When he scored his 1,000th goal, even the rival players ran to hug him. But Pelé's work didn't stop on the football field. He travelled the world, showing how the game could unite people. He played for the New York Cosmos, but only once they agreed to open training camps for disadvantaged kids. Little Pelé, who dreamt of winning the World Cup for his father, became the best football player who has ever lived. With joy and passion, he created his very own 'beautiful game', and spoke up for those in need.

'Love is more important than what we can take in life.'

Pelé

Edson Arantes do Nascimento, named after the inventor Thomas Edison, is born in the city of Três Corações in Brazil.

Ten months after his first goal, Pelé is the top scorer in the league and is put on the Brazil national football team.

Brazil's president declares Pelé an 'official national treasure' in attempts to prevent him being transferred out of the country.

1940 1956 1957 1958 1961 1965

In his first professional football match, Pelé scores a goal and his team wins the game. He buys his parents a house with his first pay cheque.

In a record that is still unbeaten, Pelé scores fifty-eight goals for his club in his first year. Over the next few years, many European clubs try to get Pelé to join them, but Pelé refuses.

Considered the world's most famous footballer at the time, Pelé performs this iconic backwards kick at a friendly international match against Belgium.

A year after finishing his third and final World Cup win with Brazil, Pelé goes to Paris to play a charity match with his team, Santos. He is driven down the Champs-Elysees, holding the World Cup trophy aloft.

Boxer Muhammad Ali embraces Pelé on the field after the footballer's last match. Pelé and Muhammad become friends, and soon begin to work together for the children's charity UNICEF.

The International Olympic Committee names Pelé the Athlete of the Century. The same year, he is named FIFA Player of the Century, and is also listed as one of the most important people of the 20th century by *TIME* magazine.

1971   1975   1977   1992   1999   2021

Pelé joins the New York Cosmos. He plays many friendly matches all over the world, often in war-torn countries, to promote unity through football.

Pelé is appointed United Nations Ambassador for Ecology and the Environment, and soon after becomes a UNESCO Goodwill Ambassador, dedicating his time to working with children who have grown up in the poverty he experienced as a boy.

Today, Pelé is considered by many to be the best footballer there has ever been, bringing joy, dance and passion to the game. He has scored over 1,000 goals in his lifetime.

Bruce Lee

ACTOR AND MARTIAL ARTIST

Born – 1940, United States
Died – 1973, Hong Kong (China)

This is the story of a little boy born in San Francisco in the year of the Dragon. His parents named him Lee Jun-Fan, but it was the hospital nurse who gave him his famous name: Bruce. He was still a young boy when his family returned to Hong Kong (China). As a child, Bruce acted in films, sometimes alongside his father, who was a well-known opera star. But he began to dream of more – he wanted to learn the secrets of Wing Chun, a type of kung fu.

He started to master the martial arts, and showed other skills, excelling in boxing, fencing and even the cha-cha. But Bruce also had a talent for street fighting. To keep him out of trouble, his parents decided to send him back to America. Before he left, Bruce made a promise to become a better person. He knew that mistakes can be forgiven, if one has the courage to admit them.

In America, Bruce finished university and set up three martial arts schools. He used his own combat method: Jeet Kune Do, a mixture of ancient kung fu, fencing, boxing and philosophy. Bruce was so fast, he once knocked out an opponent in a fight that only lasted eleven seconds! It was said he could catch a grain of rice in mid-air with his chopsticks.

Word spread, and Bruce got a part in a TV series, but he struggled to get lead acting roles. So he began to write, direct and produce his own hit movies. Finally, Hollywood gave Bruce the opportunity he had longed for – a starring role in *Enter the Dragon*, the king of kung fu movies. And by having faith in himself and never giving up, little Bruce became a hero for everyone, and the person he always dreamt he would be.

'If you love life, don't waste time, for time is what life is made up of.'

Bruce Lee

Lee Jun-Fan is born in San Francisco, California. The nurse at the hospital calls him Bruce, but he doesn't use this name until he is a teenager.

Bruce begins to act in films. At the age of nine, his first lead role is in *The Kid*, starring alongside his father.

A skilled dancer, Bruce wins the Cha-Cha Championship as well as an interschool boxing championship.

1940 1941 1949 1953 1958 1959

Bruce's family returns to Hong Kong (China), despite it being under Japanese occupation.

Bruce does poorly at school, but appears in over twenty films as a child actor, and begins to learn kung fu under esteemed martial arts expert, Master Yip Man.

To stop Bruce fighting local gangs, his parents send him to live with their friends in America, near Seattle, Washington.

140

In Seattle, Bruce teaches the Wing-Chun style of martial arts, studies philosophy at university and teaches cha-cha. Over the next three years, he opens three martial arts schools, two in California.

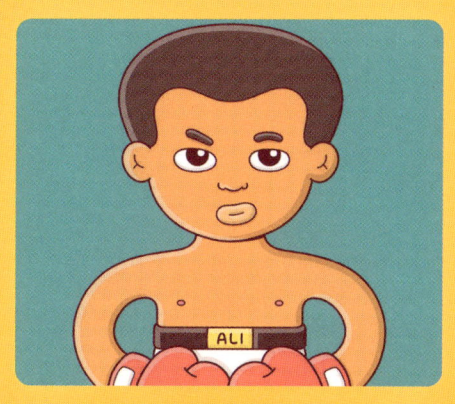

In studying moves for his own style of fighting – Jeet Kune Do, or 'The Way of the Intercepting Fist' – Bruce is influenced by boxer Muhammad Ali.

After his enormous success, Bruce is asked to star in a Hollywood film, called *Enter the Dragon*.

1961 1966 1967 1971 1973 1973

Bruce begins to play the role of Kato in the TV series *The Green Hornet*, showing his graceful fighting style.

Still not getting starring roles and unhappy about the way Asian performers are shown on films and TV, Bruce returns to Hong Kong (China). Films like *Big Boss* and *Fists of Fury* make him a true superstar.

One month before the premiere of *Enter the Dragon*, Bruce suddenly dies, aged thirty-two. The film becomes a global hit, paving the way to better roles for Asian-Americans in film and TV.

Bruce Lee

Vivienne Westwood

FASHION DESIGNER
Born – 1941, England

Little Vivienne always stood up for the outsider. When a little boy was bullied at her school, most of the children looked away and said nothing. But not Vivienne. It didn't matter what other people thought – she defended the boy when no one else would. She simply couldn't bear unfairness and unkindness. Vivienne dreamt of a world in which everyone spoke up for what was right.

When Vivienne was older, she became a teacher. But one day, she met a rebellious young man named Malcolm McLaren, and her life changed forever. He opened her eyes to a new, exhilarating world of art, politics and freedom. The couple opened a shop, mixing rock-and-roll records with fashion. Vivienne designed clothes for sale, scrawling shocking statements on T-shirts, and ripping apart old clothes before threading them with safety pins. Clothes became her way to speak out and protest. If her designs shocked people, she didn't care! Her unique style of rips and zips, slogans and safety pins, was as loud and chaotic as the music of the moment: punk. Bands took notice, and soon she was dressing the most famous punk bands of the time.

After years together, Vivienne said goodbye to Malcolm and went her own way. She began dressing artists and actresses, prime ministers and princesses. Some people said that Vivienne's outrageous clothes were unwearable, but she wasn't much interested in their opinions. Vivienne believed that fashion could make a difference to the world. She became a climate change activist, and encouraged people to buy fewer things and treasure what they have. And little Vivienne, who always stood up for what she believed in, became the most unique and outspoken fashion designer, ever. All because she believed that those who dare to speak up can change the world.

'The best fashion accessory is a book.'

Vivienne Westwood

In the middle of World War Two, Vivienne Swire is born in a little village called Tintwistle, in England.

Vivienne meets Malcolm McLaren and falls in love.

The Kings Road shop becomes a fashion mecca for the punk movement.

1941 **1958** **1965** **1971** **1970s** **1981**

Vivienne's family move to Harrow, on the outskirts of London. She works at a local factory and trains to be a teacher.

With Malcolm, Vivienne opens a shop at 430 Kings Road, selling rock-and-roll fashion. She takes apart old clothes from the 1950s to create new designs.

Vivienne and Malcolm hold their first catwalk show. They plunder ideas from the past and dress models as pirates, in frilly shirts. The show is a sensation!

1984

Vivienne leaves Malcom and goes into business by herself. People love her unique designs.

2004

The Victoria and Albert Museum in London holds an exhibition devoted to Vivienne's fabulous creations.

2014

Having spent years campaigning against climate change, Vivienne shaves off her hair as a symbol of protest. She urges people to 'Buy less, choose well, make it last'.

1980s

Iconic Vivienne Styles
- Slogan T-shirts
- Bubble skirts
- Corsets
- Tweed and tartan
- Super-high platform shoes – one model even fell over on the catwalk wearing them!

2006

Queen Elizabeth II makes Vivienne a Dame Commander of the Order of the British Empire.

2021

Vivienne continues to campaign on environmental issues and design clothes that make people feel 'grand and strong', whoever they are.

Vivienne Westwood

Bob Dylan

SINGER-SONGWRITER
Born – 1941, United States

Little Robert grew up in a small town in Minnesota. But it wasn't very exciting – he would listen to music on the radio and dream he was somewhere else. Inspired by his rock idols, Robert taught himself the guitar, the harmonica and a strange instrument called the autoharp. He experimented with rock, blues and country music, finding his voice at college with folk music. Soon, he began to compose his own songs, showing a real talent for making words fit to a beat. His songs were poetic yet powerful, and he had a new name: Bob Dylan.

Bob dropped out of college and moved to New York. There, he was a nobody. But he had his guitar, his harmonica and his hat, which he would pass around at his gigs, hoping for coins. One day, a man from a record company came to one of his gigs. Impressed by Bob's raw force and fresh lyrics, he offered him a music contract. Times were changing, and Bob's life was about to change, too.

Without trying, Bob became the voice of a generation eager for change, putting into words what millions of people felt. His songs became anthems. Although he was famous, Bob liked nothing better than working on a poem, riding on his motorcycle or talking with friends. Being an artist meant being free, and not caring about what others think.

Bob still keeps trying new sounds that challenge himself and his fans, and enjoys painting. He was the first musician to receive a Nobel Prize for Literature. In true Bob style, he didn't show up to the ceremony. Today, little Bob – one of the greatest musicians and poets of all time – feels cool just being himself. He says what he thinks and does what he likes most: dreaming up new ideas for songs and paintings.

'All I can do is be me, whoever that is.'

Bob Dylan

| 1941 | 1956 | 1959 | 1960 | 1961 | 1963 |

1941 — Robert Allen Zimmerman is born in Duluth, Minnesota, before moving to Hibbings.

1959 — At college in Minnesota, Robert starts to play folk music, now writing his own songs and using the name Bob Dylan.

1961 — Bob gets his first record contract, age twenty.

1956 — Robert teaches himself to play several instruments and enters a school talent show, but the teacher turns off the microphone when she hears his voice!

1960 — Bob drops out of college and moves to New York City, to play music.

1963 — The release of *The Freewheelin' Bob Dylan* makes Bob a household name, and a key figure in the 1960s protest movement.

Bob upsets many of his folk music fans when he plays electric guitar for the first time at the Newport Folk Festival – the crowd boos him!

Bob is inducted into the Rock & Roll Hall of Fame by Bruce Springsteen. Hundreds of singers, from Johnny Cash to Adele, continue to cover his songs.

For the first time, the Nobel Prize in Literature is given to a musician – Bob Dylan.

1965 1966 1989 2012 2016 2021

A motorcycle accident keeps Bob out of the spotlight but he continues to create several albums over the next few years, with famous songs such as 'All Along the Watchtower', covered by the likes of Jimi Hendrix.

American President Barack Obama awards Bob with the Presidential Medal of Freedom.

After selling over 100 million records and recording nearly forty albums, Bob is still writing and recording music. He paints and draws, and continues to tour, playing his 3,000th concert in 2019.

Bob Dylan

Stephen Hawking

PHYSICIST

Born – 1942, England
Died – 2018, England

Little Stephen always had a curious mind. At school, he was known as 'Einstein', like the famous scientist, but he was never top of the class – why bother with schoolwork when he could be doing something more interesting, like making a computer from clock parts and an old telephone. From an early age, Stephen used to stare up at the stars and wonder what else was out there. He dreamt of solving the mysteries of the universe.

Stephen's brilliant mind took him to England's best universities to study science. But something strange began to happen. Stephen started dropping things and tripping for no reason. Even his speech became hard to understand. At the age of twenty-one, doctors told him that a rare disease was paralysing his body and he had only two more years to live. Stephen felt like the whole universe was falling down around him... There was still so much he wanted to accomplish! He threw himself into his work with a new determination: maybe he couldn't control his body, but to study the universe all he needed was his mind.

From his wheelchair, Stephen turned his attention to black holes – some of the strangest and most powerful objects in the galaxy. He proved that they were not so black after all: there was a tiny light escaping from them. The discovery sent shockwaves through the world of science, and Stephen won many awards. When he lost the use of his voice, he had a special computer made that talked for him with a robotic drawl. He continued to study, write bestselling books and give speeches until he died – fifty-five years after his diagnosis. The little boy who became a brilliant scientist taught us all an important lesson: 'However difficult life may seem, there is always something you can do and succeed at.'

'It's a crazy world out there.
Be curious.'

Stephen Hawking

Stephen Hawking is born in Oxford, England. His birth date — January 8th, 1942 — is exactly 300 years after the death of the astronomer Galileo.

Aged seventeen, Stephen goes to Oxford University to study physics and chemistry. After graduating, he moves to Cambridge University to study for a PhD in cosmology.

Stephen marries another student called Jane, and they have three children together. Stephen gives them rides on his wheelchair!

1942 1950s 1959 1963 1965 1974

Stephen grows up in an eccentric family. His parents keep bees in the basement, make fireworks in the greenhouse and encourage their children to read books while eating dinner.

At Cambridge, Stephen receives a diagnosis of motor neurone disease (MND). People with MND gradually lose their ability to walk, talk, and eventually even swallow and breathe without help. By 1969, Stephen is using a wheelchair.

Stephen makes a discovery that changes scientists' view of the universe: he proves that matter can escape from black holes in the form of radiation (which he calls 'Hawking radiation').

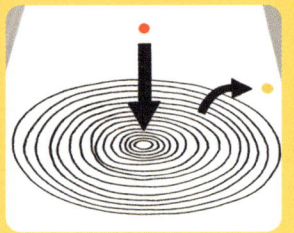

In his career, Stephen wins many awards and honours, including:
- Elected to the Royal Society (1974)
- Albert Einstein Medal (1979)
- Order of the British Empire – Commander (1982)
- Wolf Prize in Physics (1988)
- US Presidential Medal of Freedom (2009)

When Stephen's illness leaves him unable to talk, he is given a computer that talks for him. Later, he will control it using a muscle in his cheek.

To celebrate his birthday, Stephen takes a zero-gravity ride with a team of astronauts, leaving his wheelchair for the first time in forty years.

1974 1977 1985 1988 2007 2018

Stephen becomes professor of mathematics at Cambridge University, where he stays for the rest of his career.

Stephen's most famous book, *A Brief History of Time*, is published. It sells millions of copies around the world.

Stephen lives until the age of seventy-six, proving his doctors wrong.

Stephen Hawking

Muhammad Ali

BOXER, ACTIVIST AND PHILANTHROPIST

Born – 1942, United States
Died – 2016, United States

Little Cassius lived in a little house with his parents and younger brother. One day, someone stole his brand-new bicycle. He wanted to fight the thief, but a police officer told him he'd better learn to box first. Soon, Cassius was boxing in the ring, dreaming of being the greatest in the world.

As a boxer, Cassius was faster than anyone else. He pushed hard to find new ways to get quick and strong, learning martial arts moves and even boxing underwater in a swimming pool! By the age of eighteen, Cassius had won almost all of his amateur games and several boxing titles. Not long after, he won a gold medal at the Olympics in Rome. But Cassius dreamt of even more – winning the world heavyweight championship.

To tease his opponents, Cassius often used cheeky rhymes, describing how he would win... and it worked! He got his chance to fight for the heavyweight title against Sonny Liston, one of the world's toughest fighters. Everyone thought Cassius would lose, but he proved them wrong and won the champion's belt.

Cassius was not just a famous boxer, but a courageous defender of African-American rights. Inspired by the teachings of Islam, he changed his name to Muhammad Ali, an Arabic name that made him feel strong and proud to be himself. When the US entered the Vietnam War in the 1960s, Muhammad refused to fight in the conflict. He was stripped of his title and banned from boxing for three years.

When Muhammad returned to the ring, he made it big, becoming the first boxer to win the heavyweight belt three times. After retiring, Muhammad spent the rest of his life working for charities, helping others. Since then, many young boxers have followed in Muhammad's steps – the little boy who dreamt of being 'the greatest'.

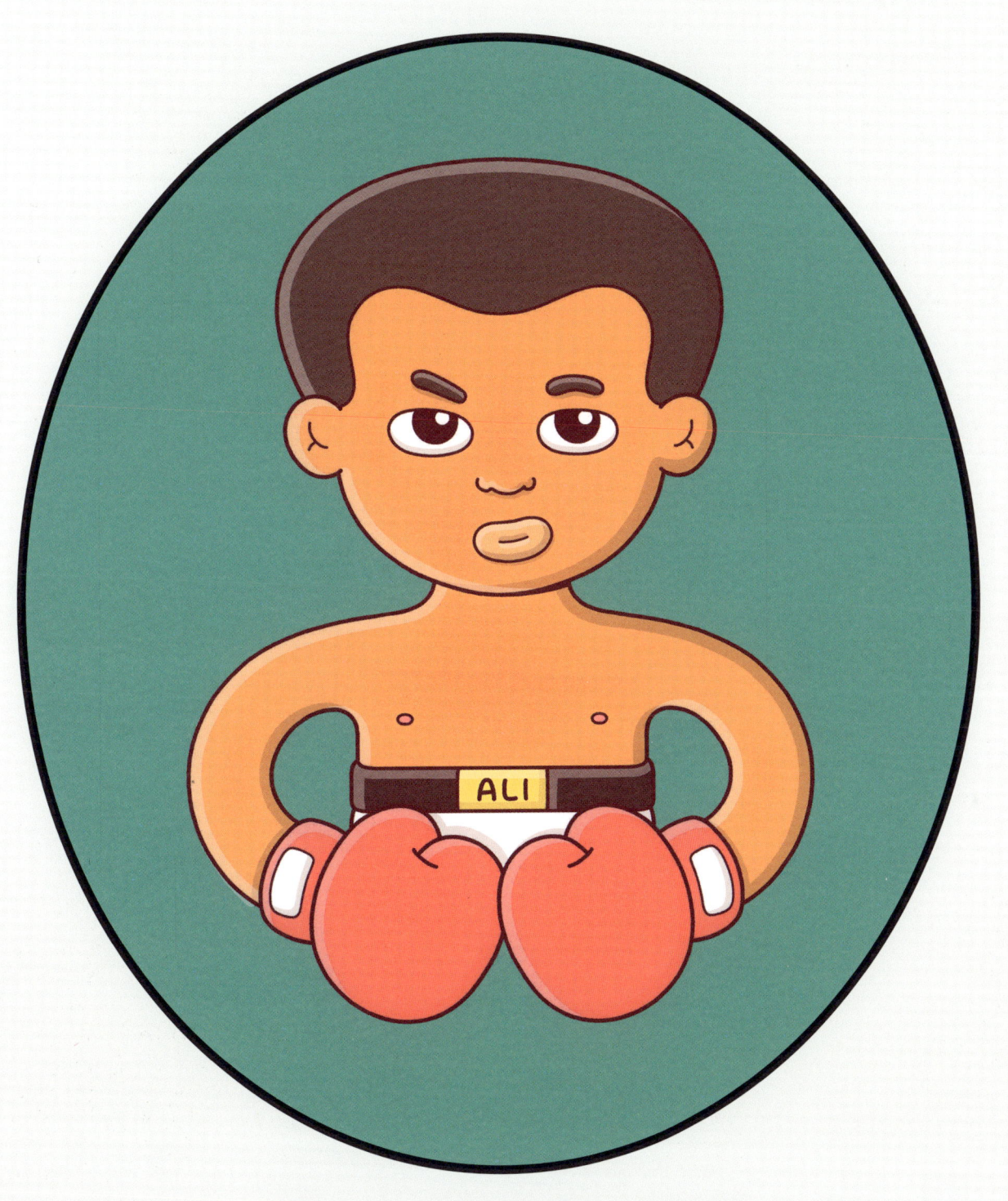

'Don't count the days, make the days count.'

Muhammad Ali

Cassius Marcellus Clay, Jr. is born and raised in Louisville, Kentucky.

Aged eighteen, Cassius brings home a gold medal in the light heavyweight division for boxing at the 1960 Olympics in Rome.

Cassius changes his name to Muhammad Ali, to reflect his new Islamic faith. He converts to orthodox Islam in the 1970s.

1942 1954 1960 1964 1964 1965

When Cassius is twelve, someone steals his bicycle. The police officer on duty suggests he should come to his boxing class and learn how to fight.

Aged twenty-two, Cassius wins his first heavyweight title against the favourite, Sonny Liston. From then on, Cassius is a formidable fighter. He is fast, smart and uses slick rhymes to taunt his opponents.

Muhammad defends his title against Floyd Patterson, former heavyweight champion.

Muhammad is arrested, stripped of his title and banned from boxing for three years after refusing to fight in the Vietnam War. He doesn't believe in the war, and thinks it is unfair that Black people are expected to fight in the war, yet are still treated unequally in America.

Muhammad defeats heavyweight champion George Foreman in Kinshasa, Zaire. The 'Rumble in the Jungle' becomes the world's most-watched live TV broadcast, seen by about one billion people!

Muhammad receives the Presidential Medal of Freedom from President George W. Bush. Later that year, he opens the Muhammad Ali Center in Louisville, where visitors can learn about his career and beliefs.

1967 1971 1974 1976 2005 2016

Muhammad's conviction is overturned. With his boxing ban lifted, he loses to rival Joe Frazier in what is called the 'Fight of the Century'. But he wins at their next fight, four years later, at the 'Thrilla in Manila' in the Philippines.

Muhammad uses the 'Accupunch' to knock out an opponent. He learnt the move from Taekwondo Grandmaster Jhoon Rhee, who himself was taught it by martial art expert Bruce Lee.

Having lived for many years with Parkinson's disease, Muhammad dies in Phoenix, Arizona, at the age of seventy-four.

Muhammad Ali

Aretha Franklin

SINGER AND CIVIL RIGHTS ACTIVIST

Born – 1942, United States
Died – 2018, United States

If there was someone in Detroit who was born to sing, it was little Aretha. Her mother was a gospel singer and her father was a preacher who believed in the healing power of music. Aretha's home was always filled with musicians and she learnt to play the piano just by listening to them. Soon, she started singing in the church's gospel choir where her father was a minister. Listening to Aretha's voice, so powerful and smooth, made everyone feel that tomorrow would be a brighter day.

Aretha's father took her on tour, and together they went from church to church. Wherever Aretha performed, she did it with such grace that people would cry with joy. But Aretha dreamt that her voice could be heard outside the church. When a record company offered her a contract, she didn't have to think about it twice. Before long, Aretha's songs were climbing the charts. One of these was called 'Respect', written by singer Otis Redding. It became an anthem for African-American women demanding equal rights.

Once she was a star, Aretha started writing her own songs and producing them, too. She recorded hundreds of great hits, writing about everyday ups and downs, and singing from the bottom of her heart. That's what soul was all about!

When Aretha was inducted into the Rock & Roll Hall of Fame, she was the first woman in history to be on the list. But her greatest honour was singing at the inauguration of Barack Obama, the first African-American President of the United States – she was the voice of one of the most important moments in history! To this day, no one can sing a song quite like Aretha, the little girl who won the R-E-S-P-E-C-T of millions and became the true Queen of Soul.

'Every birthday is a gift.
Every day is a gift.'

Aretha Franklin

Aretha Louise Franklin is born in Memphis, Tennessee.

Accompanied by her father, Aretha begins touring, performing gospel music in churches around America.

After moving to a different record label, Aretha makes even more chart-topping songs, which turns her into a household name.

1942   1952   1954   1960   1966   1967

Not long after her mother's death, Aretha joins her father's gospel choir at their church.

Aretha leaves Detroit for New York City and signs to a record label, releasing several albums and singles that make it into the charts.

Aretha's signature song, 'Respect', is released, and is hailed as an anthem for equal rights.

Aretha wins her first two Grammys, after a string of hit singles and top-selling albums.

Aretha becomes the first female to be inducted into the Rock & Roll Hall of Fame.

Aretha sings at the inauguration of Barack Obama, America's first African-American President.

1968   1968   1987   1998   2009   2018

Civil rights leader Martin Luther King, Jr. is assassinated and Aretha sings at her friend's funeral.

When Luciano Pavarotti is too ill to sing the opera aria 'Nessun dorma' at the Grammy Awards, he asks his friend Aretha to step in. It is seen on TV by over one billion people.

Aretha dies at her home in Detroit, Michigan, aged seventy-six.

Aretha Franklin

Billie Jean King

TENNIS PLAYER AND ACTIVIST
Born – 1943, United States

Little Billie Jean was born on the sunny coast of California. She loved all sports, but when she discovered tennis, it was love at first serve! From the first time she played, Billie Jean dreamt of being a champion. Determined to be the best player on the planet, Billie Jean began showing up at drop-in lessons offered by a professional tennis player. He became her first coach and she became his best pupil ever.

One day, at a tournament, Billie Jean was pushed aside from a team picture because she was wearing shorts, not a skirt. But that wasn't all… there were no sports scholarships for girls in college, and women received smaller prizes than men for winning the same tournaments. Billie Jean fought this, and along with eight other bold tennis players, she helped create the Women's Tennis Association, working for equal pay and opportunities. The day the first sports scholarships were given to women, Billie Jean felt on top of the world.

In one single season, Billie Jean won three Grand Slams, the most important tournaments in the world. She became the first tennis player and the first woman to be named Sports Person of the Year. But many male players still looked down on female players. This came to a head when fifty-five-year-old Bobby Riggs, a retired tennis champion, challenged Billie Jean, saying it would be easy to win against a woman, even the current female champion. Billie Jean quickly beat him, in a turning point for equal rights in tennis. Later, she helped start a league where everyone would play together, regardless of gender. Billie Jean continues to stand up for equal rights and has proved to be not only a world tennis champion – but somebody who dreamt of changing things, and did.

'The main thing is to care. Care very hard, even if it is only a game you are playing.'

Billie Jean King

Billie Jean Moffitt is born in Long Beach, California to a family of athletes.

Not long after buying her first tennis racquet, Billie Jean joins a drop-in free session with tennis player Clyde Walker – he becomes her coach.

Aged seventeen, Billie Jean is part of the youngest pair, alongside Karen Hantze, to win the Wimbledon women's doubles.

1943   1953   1957   1959   1961   1966

At first, Billie Jean loves playing baseball. But she realises that she won't be able to play as a professional when she grows up – there aren't any women's teams.

Billie Jean makes her Grand Slam debut at the US Championships at age fifteen.

After winning the Wimbledon women's singles championship, Billie Jean becomes a star around the world. She wins match after match to become World No. 1 in women's tennis.

164

To protest against unfairness, Billie Jean and eight other female players agree to be paid just $1 to play in a women-only tournament! Over the next few years, Billie Jean helps woman athletes to get college sports scholarships.

Bobby Riggs challenges Billie Jean to a tennis match. She wins and the 'Battle of the Sexes' goes down in history as the match that changed tennis.

American President Barack Obama gives Billie Jean the Presidential Medal of Freedom for standing up for gender equality and LGBTQ+ rights.

1970   1973   1973   1987   2009   2021

Billie Jean helps found the Women's Tennis Association, and fights for male and female players to be paid equally. A few months later, the US Open becomes the first major tournament to offer equal prize money to men and women.

Billie Jean's tennis partner, Ilana Kloss, becomes her life partner. Together, they promote mixed-gender team tennis.

After winning thirty-nine Grand Slams and several awards, Billie Jean is recognised as one of the most exciting tennis players of all time. She continues to work for equality and LGBTQ+ rights and teaches young players the value of teamwork.

Billie Jean King

Dolly Parton

SINGER-SONGWRITER, ACTOR AND PHILANTHROPIST

Born – 1946, United States

Little Dolly grew up in the foothills of Tennessee's Great Smoky Mountains with her eleven siblings. She didn't have much, but she was gifted with a lovely voice – and that was worth more than any treasure. She began to write songs on her guitar and perform them for whoever would listen. Singing barefoot on the front porch, Dolly dreamt of jumping onstage in high heels.

Dolly's uncle Bill was amazed by her talent and helped her to get started in the music business. She was just ten years old when she got a regular slot singing for a local radio station, fitting it in alongside school. Later, Dolly moved to Nashville, the city of music. With her soulful voice and songwriting talent, she was ready to become a star. So, when Porter Wagoner – a famous country music entertainer – asked Dolly to sing with him, she didn't hesitate. Together, they topped the charts. But Dolly also wrote many moving songs about being a woman, and earned herself loyal fans. It was time for her to go solo.

Dolly's own songs were a great success, but she wanted new adventures. She crossed over into pop music and began acting in films. With her unique voice and fabulous image, she became a total superstar, winning several awards and topping the charts. Wanting to use her fame and wealth to help others, Dolly started a special library that sent books to kids in need. And she didn't stop there. Dolly built a theme park and became one of the most successful women in show business. She now owns radio stations, TV channels and record companies, too. And after fifty years onstage, little Dolly has become one of the most respected country performers of all time – a larger-than-life living legend, with a heart as big as her dreams.

'Being a star just means that you just find your own special place.'

Dolly Parton

Dolly is born in Pittman Center, Tennessee, near the Great Smoky Mountains – one of twelve children.

Aged thirteen, Dolly records her first single, 'Puppy Love' and appears at the Grand Ole Opry, where she meets country music legend, Johnny Cash.

Famous country musician, Porter Wagoner, invites Dolly to join his weekly TV show. They go on to make several Top 10 singles together.

1946 1955 1959 1964 1967 1974

By the age of ten, Dolly is singing on the local radio station and performing for TV in Knoxville, Tennessee.

The day after finishing high school, Dolly moves to Nashville, Tennessee, writing songs for other musicians.

Dolly's solo career finally takes off, with hits 'Jolene', 'I Will Always Love You' and 'Love is Like a Butterfly'. She leaves Wagoner's TV show.

Dolly wins the first of her eleven Grammies for her song 'Here You Come Again' and is named entertainer of the year by the Country Music Awards.

Away from the stage, Dolly opens a theme park called Dollywood, which centres on Appalachian traditions, in the Great Smoky Mountains of Tennessee, where she grew up.

Dolly's charity 'Dolly Parton's Imagination Library' sends out its 100 millionth free book to a child, and is honoured by the American Library of Congress.

1978   1980   1986   1987   2018   2021

Dolly appears in the successful comedy *Nine to Five*, also writing its Academy-Award-nominated theme song. She goes on to act in several films and TV series over the years.

With country music singers Emmylou Harris and Linda Ronstadt, Dolly releases *Trio*. The album sells several million copies, and Dolly tops the charts again.

Dolly donates $1 million towards vaccine development for Covid-19 while continuing to entertain her fans online. She remains one of the most-honoured and loved female country performers of all time, having penned over 3,000 songs and earned eleven Grammy Awards out of fifty nominations.

Dolly Parton

David Bowie

SINGER-SONGWRITER

Born – 1947, England
Died – 2016, United States

Little David didn't care about fitting in with the crowd. In the tiny house in London where he grew up, his older brother Terry played him jazz and rock music. David would spend hours listening to records – he was so inspired by what he heard that he started dreaming up ideas that were out of this world. Sometimes David's schoolteachers weren't sure if he was a boy or a girl, but David wasn't bothered about what other people thought. He believed in his own expression, unique to anyone else. He had a real talent for singing and mastered many instruments – and his dance moves were from another planet!

After leaving school, David began making music and writing his own songs. He jumped from band to band looking for a chance, and dreamt that – one day – all the lonely kids on Planet Earth would sing his songs out loud. Changing his name to David Bowie, he decided to go solo. His first hit song, about a lonely astronaut, was played over television footage of the first man walking on the moon. And David's career took off!

David began performing as his alien alter-ego, Ziggy Stardust, complete with a red quiff, face paint and wild outfits. He was the coolest space invader the world had ever seen. David became a true superstar – never boring, and always reinventing himself. He inspired generations of fans to find their own voice and dare to be different.

David continued to make music, filled with futuristic sounds, for the rest of his life. By never being afraid to be himself, little David became the most unique star who ever fell to Earth. He left the world as one of the most iconic singer-songwriters and performers of his generation.

'Tomorrow belongs to those who can hear it coming.'

David Bowie

David Robert Jones is born in Brixton, London, before moving at the age of six to Bromley on the London-Kent border.

David leaves school at sixteen and plays in a band called The Konrads with his friend George. Soon, he goes solo and begins to find fame with his own songs.

David studies dramatic arts and mime with choreographer Lindsay Kemp, and learns to use make-up and costume to great effect on stage.

1947 1962 1963 1965 1968 1969

During a fistfight, David's friend George punches him in the eye, leaving David with a damaged pupil that gives him a distinctive look – one eye dark, the other blue.

David changes his surname to Bowie, after the 19th-century pioneer James Bowie.

'Space Oddity', David's first hit, is played over the UK television footage of the Apollo 11 moon landing, which saw the first person walk on the moon.

Ziggy Stardust, David's new character, emerges, with a new album and band, along with otherworldly hair, costumes and make-up.

To take a break from America, David moves to West Berlin in Germany for three years. His recording studio is near the now-demolished Berlin Wall.

David receives the Lifetime Achievement Award at the Grammys in the USA.

1972   1975   1976   1986   2006   2016

David meets and becomes great friends with John Lennon, collaborating on the song 'Fame', David's first No. 1 hit in the charts in the USA.

David stars in *Labyrinth*, a fantasy adventure film that is now considered a cult classic.

Two days after the release of his 26th album, *Darkstar*, David dies, aged sixty-nine.

David Bowie

Elton John

Zaha Hadid

Evonne Goolagong

Steve Jobs

Prince

Ayrton Senna

Jean-Michel Basquiat

Mindy Kaling

Malala Yousafzai

Greta Thunberg

1947
–
2003

Elton John

SINGER-SONGWRITER

Born – 1947, England

In the suburbs of London, a little boy named Reggie started playing his grandmother's piano. Soon enough, he could pick out tunes by ear. From that day on, whenever his parents argued, music became his refuge. Reggie attended London's Royal Academy of Music, singing and performing with other musicians. Inspired by the music of Little Richard and Ray Charles, he began playing in bands and dreamt of being a star.

Everything clicked when he met Bernie Taupin. With Reggie providing the melody and Bernie writing the words, the pair were making beautiful songs together in no time. After two years of composing and playing songs for other artists, Reggie gave himself a new name and a new wardrobe, with enormous glasses, feathers and sequins – Elton John was born! One morning, Elton and Bernie wrote a song at breakfast, called 'Your Song'. Almost overnight, Elton was a superstar.

On stage, Elton could be anything he dreamt. He could make the crowd sing, dance, laugh and cry. When he pulled his signature handstand on his piano, it felt like the whole room was floating up with him. But once the shows were over, Elton felt terribly alone. This changed when he met a boy who was ill in hospital. Ryan showed him that life is too wonderful to waste. The day they said goodbye, Elton promised to honour his friend's memory by being his best self. He began taking better care of himself. And now, with his husband David Furnish and their two children, Elton doesn't feel alone. He has the family he always wanted.

After a long life dedicated to music and to helping those in need, Elton John still remembers little Reggie, the shy boy who sought comfort at his piano, and dreamt of bringing happiness to the world with his songs.

'Music has a healing power. It has the ability to take people out of themselves for a few hours.'

Elton John

1947 — Reggie Kenneth Dwight is born in Middlesex, England.

1951 — At his grandmother's house, Reggie picks out the melody of Winifred Atwell's 'The Skater's Waltz' without the use of sheet music.

1958 — Reggie wins a scholarship to attend the Royal Academy of Music in London, after repeating the piece he hears the teacher practising at his audition.

1964 — Reggie forms a band, Bluesology, and leaves the Royal Academy before taking his final exams.

1967 — Answering an ad in the paper, Reggie goes to an audition and meets songwriter Bernie Taupin. Together, they begin to write for other artists. Reggie changes his name to Elton John.

1969 — With a new look of bright and exciting outfits and glittery, large glasses, Elton makes his first album, *Empty Sky*, still writing with Bernie.

Elton's second album turns him into a star, with his first hit single 'Your Song'. Over the next few years, Elton and Bernie create hit after hit.

Elton is inducted into the Rock & Roll Hall of Fame. He also wins a Grammy and an Academy Award for his soundtrack work on the film *The Lion King*.

With playwright Lee Hall, Elton composes the music for *Billy Elliot the Musical*, seen by over eleven million people around the world.

1970 1975 1994 1998 2005 2018

After becoming great friends with tennis champion Billie Jean King, Elton writes a song in her honour, called 'Philadelphia Freedom'. It becomes a No. 1 single.

For his charitable work, Elton is knighted by Queen Elizabeth II.

Elton quits touring to spend more time with his husband and two kids. With thirty-one top-ten hits and countless awards, he remains one of the world's best-loved singers and an LGBTQ+ icon.

Elton John

Zaha Hadid

ARCHITECT

Born – 1950, Iraq
Died – 2016, United States

Little Zaha always had a mind of her own, even when she was young. Zaha knew what she wanted, and she liked to do things her way. One day, an architect friend of the family came to their house in Baghdad, carrying his drawings and models. Zaha was fascinated by the beautiful shapes and lines. From then on, she began to design her own clothes and bedroom furniture, making them just the way she liked them. As she dreamt big dreams of the future, she knew she would be an architect.

Growing up, Zaha visited faraway towns and cities, and drew everything she saw. With her father, she travelled to ancient Sumer in southern Iraq, where the buildings, landscape and people all seemed to flow together. Zaha realised she wanted to design buildings that did the same.

When Zaha moved to London to study architecture, her one-of-a-kind ideas amazed her teachers. Her building designs weren't boring squares or rectangles, but bold, curved shapes that looked like they were moving and alive! After she started work, Zaha dreamt up daring, experimental designs for buildings, but none of them were built – people said they were too radical, too difficult. But Zaha refused to compromise. I'll prove them wrong, she thought. And she did.

Over the next twenty years, Zaha used the power of computers to build what people had said was unbuildable, and her curvy buildings sprung up around the world, from Beirut to Beijing. She became known as the 'Queen of Curve', and won prize after prize, year after year. In an industry run by men, she changed the way that people thought about women, especially an Arab woman. And determined little Zaha became one of the most successful architects of her time – a true pioneer, who dared to dream and build the impossible.

'There are 360 degrees, so why stick to one?'

Zaha Hadid

Zaha, a Muslim girl, is born in Baghdad. Her mother is an artist, and her father a wealthy industrialist and politician.

When she is old enough, Zaha goes to boarding school in England and Switzerland. At university she studies mathematics.

When she graduates, Zaha remains at the AA School as a teacher.

1950 **1950s** **1960s** **1972** **1977** **1979**

Zaha attends a prestigious Catholic school, where children of all religions are welcome. Her favourite classes are mathematics and art.

Zaha moves to London to study at the Architectural Association (AA) School. She wows her tutors with her new ideas.

Zaha opens her own architecture practice. Her early designs win many competitions but are thought impossible to build.

Finally, the first of Zaha's buildings is completed – Vitra Fire Station in Germany. Over the next twenty years, Zaha designs museums, cultural centres, sports stadiums, a school and even a ski jump!

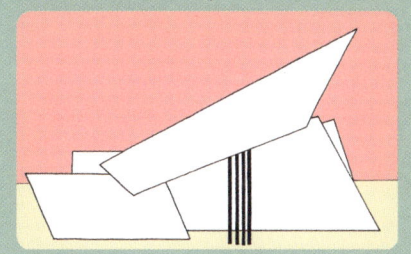

A pair of shoes designed by Zaha is launched at London Fashion Week. Zaha also designs jewellery, bags and furniture.

One of Zaha's most iconic designs is completed – the Heydar Aliyev Centre in Baku, Azerbaijan.

1993   2004   2008   2012   2013   2016

Zaha is awarded the Pritzker Prize, architecture's highest honour. She's the first woman and the first Muslim to win the prize.

Queen Elizabeth II makes Zaha a Dame Commander of the Order of the British Empire.

Zaha dies, aged sixty-five. She is remembered today as a trailblazer for women in architecture.

Zaha Hadid

Evonne Goolagong

TENNIS PLAYER
Born – 1951, Australia

Little Evonne grew up on a hot, dusty farm in Australia. Her family was descended from the Wiradjuri people, who had lived on the land for more than 60,000 years. Evonne's family couldn't afford many toys, but one day, Evonne found the most amazing treasure: an old tennis ball. Evonne began reading about a young female tennis player who went to England to play on Wimbledon's magical centre court. She went to bed dreaming about one day playing there.

At this time in Australia, Indigenous Australians were treated very poorly by white people, who wouldn't let them enjoy many everyday things that white people did, including playing tennis. But Evonne went to the tennis club every day, peeking through the fence, watching games and memorising everything the coach said. Finally, the club's manager gave her the key to the court so she could teach herself how to play after hours. And she did! She was super fast and had an amazing ability to judge a tennis ball's speed and bounce.

A well-known tennis coach heard about Evonne's talent. When she was just fifteen, she moved to Sydney to train to become a professional player. The day she left home, Evonne's mother told her: 'Do not worry about winning or losing, just play your best and have a lovely time.' It became Evonne's secret weapon – she enjoyed her matches, not afraid to lose.

Shot after shot, Evonne made it into all the major tournaments, ending up at her dream court – Wimbledon. She won there and became number one in the world. After winning ninety-two tournaments, Evonne retired. But she continues to inspire with her charitable work, helping Indigenous children to make it onto the court. She is a national treasure of Australia, not afraid to break through barriers, on and off the courts.

'Your dreams when you are little are the force that keeps you going.'

Evonne Goolagong

1951 — Evonne Goolagong is born in Barellan, New South Wales, Australia.

1953 — After finding a tennis ball under the wheel of her father's car, Evonne becomes obsessed with hitting it against a wall using a racquet made by her father.

1959 — Evonne begins to play at her local tennis club, but is only allowed in after the white people have left.

1965 — Evonne moves to Sydney, to train and live with her tennis coach's family. She becomes Junior Australian Champion.

1971 — Within five years, Evonne realises her dream to play at Wimbledon in England. She beats fellow Australian Margaret Court to become the No. 1 female tennis player in the world, aged twenty.

1973 — In the Wimbledon semi-finals, Evonne loses to eventual winner Billie Jean King.

Evonne wins Wimbledon again, this time with her young daughter watching from the stands. She becomes the first mother to win the tournament in more than sixty years.

Evonne is appointed captain of the Australian Fed Cup team.

Evonne is awarded Companion of the Order of Australia, and the International Tennis Federation presents her with its highest accolade, the Philippe Chatrier Award.

1980   1983   2002   2005   2018   2021

Although she retires from playing tennis professionally, Evonne continues to teach, raising her family and moving to America.

Inspired to help further the dreams of Indigenous youth in Australia, Evonne sets up and runs the Goolagong National Development Camp for Indigenous boys and girls.

Evonne, who has won ninety-two tournaments, endless awards, titles and accolades, continues to advocate for women in tennis and Indigenous rights.

Evonne Goolagong

Steve Jobs

ENTREPRENEUR AND INVENTOR

Born – 1955, United States
Died – 2011, United States

Little Steve was born in San Francisco. He loved nothing better than working with his dad in the garage, taking things apart and finding out how they were made. One summer, he joined a club run by an electronics company, where he stumbled across a mysterious machine that he had never seen before: a computer, big enough to fill a room. Steve fell in love with the possibility of this amazing machine – the most awesome tool ever invented! He dreamt of a future where computers could change people's lives for the better.

At school, some people thought Steve was a geek, and others thought he was a hippy. But Steve was just himself. He could talk about electronics for hours with his friend Woz, but he also loved art, literature and philosophy. One day, he went to see Woz, who was busy working on a home-made computer. Wouldn't it be great, Steve wondered, if every person could have a simple, easy-to-use computer in their own home? So, Steve and Woz decided to start a business together. They named their company 'Apple', and Steve's garage became their headquarters. The two friends spent long days and nights programming and imagining what a 'personal computer' might look like. Steve was the visionary, and Woz was the genius engineer.

Soon, they went from selling two hundred computers to becoming one of America's top tech companies. Steve hired the most talented artists, designers and engineers, and challenged them to think differently to create the most extraordinary devices – not just computers, but music players and mobile phones. He didn't just want his products to be great – he wanted them to be 'insanely great'! And little Steve became one of the most successful entrepreneurs the world has ever seen – a visionary of technology, who had the courage to follow his heart and his intuition.

'Don't let the noise of others' opinions drown out your own inner voice.'

Steve Jobs

1955 — Steve is born in San Francisco, California. He is adopted as a baby by Paul and Clara Jobs.

1967 — At a summer camp, twelve-year-old Steve falls in love with computers. At that time, they are enormous – as big as a room!

1972 — After high school, Steve goes to Reed College in Oregon, but finds the classes boring and drops out.

1960s — Each day after school, Steve joins his dad in his workshop, where they dismantle everyday items to see how they work.

1968 — Steve becomes friends with Steve Wozniak ('Woz'), who is a few years older than him. They bond over a love for electronics.

1974 — Steve takes a job with the video game maker Atari and saves money to travel. He visits India, where he studies the religion of Zen Buddhism.

Back home, Steve meets up with Woz, who is designing his own personal computer. Steve suggests they go into business together.

In his speech introducing the Apple Macintosh (Mac) computer, Steve quotes a song by Bob Dylan – one of his heroes.

Steve rejoins Apple. Under his leadership, it branches out into new, successful products, including:
- iMac computer (1998)
- iTunes music software (2001)
- iPod music player (2001)
- iPhone (2007)
- iPad tablet (2010)

1974   1976   1984   1985   1997   2011

The friends set up a company, Apple Computer, and release the Apple 1 computer. The next year they release the Apple II, which is very successful. The company grows rapidly.

Steve leaves Apple and sets up his own company called NeXT. It buys Pixar, which Steve builds up into a successful animation studio – its first film is *Toy Story*. Pixar's success makes Steve a billionaire.

Steve dies from cancer, aged fifty-six, leaving behind one of the most successful technology companies of all time.

Steve Jobs

Prince

SINGER AND MUSICIAN

Born – 1958, United States
Died – 2016, United States

Born into a household of jazz musicians, little Prince fell in love with the power of music from an early age. Sneaking onto his dad's piano, he wrote his first song aged seven, and could play the drums and guitar not long after. At school, Prince took as many music classes as he could, while also training in ballet and modern dance at the Minnesota Dance Theatre. He dreamt of being a performer like funk superstar James Brown, combining music and dance in exciting new ways.

As soon as he finished high school, Prince flew to New York to find a record deal. It didn't take him long. Just a year later, he was in a recording studio in California, writing, composing, singing... and playing all twenty-seven instruments for his first album! But it was his next album, *Prince*, that made him a true star. He won awards, starred in films and had top-selling album after album.

No matter what he did, Prince made his own rules... and then broke them all, just because he could! He tried blues, rock, pop and funk, blending them together. On stage, he loved to express himself, dancing all over the stage and wearing high heels and eye-catching outfits. For many of his songs, he sang in a very high voice, sometimes even screaming!

For some time, Prince changed his name to a symbol that united the feminine and masculine side. He was known as 'The Artist Formerly Known as Prince': a free spirit who no one dared to label. His determination and honesty inspired others to find their own, authentic expression. And 1,000 songs later, little Prince showed the world that life is a beautiful rainbow of colour... where you are free to dream and there is no limit to what you can try and do.

'A strong spirit transcends rules.'

Prince

1958 — Prince Rogers Nelson is born in Minneapolis, Minnesota. His mother is a jazz singer and his father a jazz pianist.

1971 — Prince trains in dance and classical ballet at the Minnesota Dance Theatre, thanks to a programme at his school.

1972 — Aged fourteen, Prince joins his first band, playing drums and guitar as well as piano.

1972 — After his parents divorce, Prince is taken to a James Brown concert by his stepfather, who is also a musician. It changes the way Prince thinks of performing and is a great influence on his style to come.

1977 — Prince makes his first demo of his music to send to record companies. Within a year, he is recording his first album in California for a record label.

1982 — Prince's album, *1999*, sells over four million copies, becomes an international hit and earns Prince his first Grammy nomination.

Prince stars in *Purple Rain*, a film based partly on his own life, and releases the *Purple Rain* album – both film and album reach No. 1 in the USA at the same time, and he wins an Academy Award for Best Original Song Score.

Prince changes his name to a symbol that is meant to represent both the feminine and masculine side of all of us. He identifies as both male and female, celebrating the qualities of both.

On his final tour, Prince covers David Bowie's song 'Heroes', in memory of the singer's recent death.

1984   1989   1993   2007   2016   2016

Prince's soundtrack for the movie *Batman* is released to great acclaim – it goes on to reach No. 1 in the charts.

Over 140 million TV viewers watch Prince perform during the halftime show of the Super Bowl, held in Miami, Florida that year. His performance is called 'the best Super Bowl performance ever' by *Billboard* magazine.

Prince dies suddenly at his home in Minnesota, aged fifty-seven. The city of Minneapolis hosts an all-night dance party in the streets that night to celebrate his life.

Ayrton Senna

> **RACING DRIVER**
>
> Born – 1960, Brazil
> Died – 1994, Italy

Little Ayrton was four when his father built him a go-kart to play with. But for him, it was not just a toy. It was his dream. When he started the engine and set off, it was like he had been driving his whole life. At Ayrton's first official go-kart race, most of the drivers were twice his age. They couldn't believe their eyes when a thirteen-year-old beat them all! Ayrton was not always the winner, but defeat offered a chance to learn something new. Once, after losing a race due to the rain, he spent days practising, even forgetting to show up for dinner. It became his special skill to race well in the rain.

Leaving his friends and family, Ayrton went to England to follow his dream of driving with Formula One – the highest level of race-car driving in the world. Within three years, he had made it onto a Formula One team. One of his teammates was a French driver called Alain Prost. Their rivalry became legendary. In their first season, Ayrton ended up winning one more race than Alain, and he was crowned as the world champion!

Japan, Monaco, San Marino... Wherever Ayrton raced, he memorised the circuit, knowing each curve of the track like the back of his hand. Ayrton's mechanics loved reading his reports, which were full of little tips and big ideas. Ayrton always helped fellow racers who had crashed, and looked for ways to improve safety on the track. Off the track, he gave huge amounts of money and support to people, especially children. Today, whenever the engines roar at the circuit and a new race begins, the crowds remember little Ayrton – the bold, bright kid loved by millions, who dreamt of being the greatest driver of all time.

'The harder I push, the more I find within myself.'

Ayrton Senna

Ayrton Senna is born to wealthy parents in Sao Paulo, Brazil.

Ayrton learns how to drive a car, perching on the edge of the seat to reach the steering wheel.

When he is seventeen, Ayrton wins the South American Kart Championship.

1960   1964   1967   1973   1977   1981

Using an old lawnmower, Ayrton's father builds him a go-cart. Soon, four-year-old Ayrton is zooming around the streets of his neighbourhood.

Ayrton moves to England to try and make his way onto a professional racing team. He wins the British Formula Ford 1600 championship and, two years later, the British Formula Three Championship.

Entering his first karting competition at the age of thirteen, Ayrton manages to surprise many of the older drivers with his skill.

After testing for Formula One teams, Ayrton joins a new team called Toleman.

Ayrton wins the Formula One World Driver's Championship, and again in 1990 and 1991.

During a practice run at Spa-Francorchamps in Belgium, Érik Comas crashes at high speed. Ayrton jumps out of his car and runs to his friend, helping him until medics arrive. After this, Ayrton works hard to improve safety in Formula One racing.

1984 1985 1988 1991 1992 1994

At the Portuguese Grand Prix, Ayrton wins his first race with Formula One, in very wet conditions. He considers it to be the best drive of his career.

At the Brazilian Grand Prix, Ayrton manages to win the race despite serious car problems. He is so exhausted, he has to be helped out of the car!

In the San Marino Grand Prix in Italy, Ayrton dies in a car crash. His charity work carries on in the form of the Ayrton Senna Institute.

Ayrton Senna

JEAN-MICHEL BASQUIAT

PAINTER

Born – 1960, United States
Died – 1988, United States

Little Jean-Michel was just four when he started drawing, eager to show the world what he could do. He loved visiting museums and spent long afternoons drawing cartoons, dreaming of the great artist he would become. 'Papa, I'm going to be famous,' little Jean-Michel announced to his father one day. And why not? It was a big dream, but he had a big talent.

One day, Jean-Michel was hit by a car. While he lay in bed recovering, his mother gave him a present: an anatomy book. The little boy was spellbound by the drawings of skeletons and skulls, teeth and tendons. One day I'll paint this, he promised himself.

When his mother became ill, Jean-Michel's world turned upside down – he dropped out of school and ran away. But he found a home at City-As-School, an unconventional school where he met other artists like him. He began spray-painting art on buildings and subway trains. More and more people started talking about this talented teenage graffiti artist. Almost in the blink of an eye, everything changed for Jean-Michel. One year he was selling hand-painted postcards to make a living; the next he was the brightest new star of the New York art scene.

Jean-Michel's paintings were unlike anything seen before. They mixed images, words and symbols into a bold, beautiful mess that people fell in love with. His art was inspired by the things he had loved as a child – comic book art, and the old anatomy book his mother had given him. Jean-Michel painted portraits of ordinary people, and used his art to speak boldly about issues such as racism. And the boy who dreamt he would be famous became one of the most important artists of his time, and changed people's ideas about what art could be, forever.

'I like kids' work more than work by real artists any day.'

JEAN-MICHEL BASQUIAT

Jean-Michel is born in Brooklyn, New York, to a Puerto Rican mother and Haitian father. He can read, write and draw by the age of four.

Recovering from an accident, seven-year-old Jean-Michel is given *Gray's Anatomy* as a gift. The famous textbook was first published in 1858.

Jean-Michel drops out of school when he dumps a box of shaving cream on the principal's head for a dare!

1960 **1960s** **1968** **1976** **1977** **1978**

With his mother, Jean-Michel visits museums in Manhattan. At the age of six, he is a Junior Member of the Brooklyn Museum.

After his mother becomes unwell, and his parents divorce, Jean-Michel moves to City-As-School, a non-traditional school for gifted New York children. Here, he meets other artists like him — including Al Diaz.

With Al, Jean-Michel starts spray-painting buildings in downtown New York, signed with a made-up name: SAMO.

Jean-Michel's work appears in an art show for the first time – he is just nineteen.

Jean-Michel has his first solo art exhibition in New York. His paintings now sell for tens of thousands of dollars.

The New York Times Magazine puts Jean-Michel on the front cover. He is a superstar.

1980   1981   1982   1984   1985   1988

Jean-Michel meets one of his idols, the famous pop artist Andy Warhol. After their first lunch, Jean-Michel goes home and within two hours has sent Andy a still-wet painting of the two of them! It's the start of a great friendship.

Jean-Michel and Andy Warhol start to work on lots of art together – and go to lots of parties, too!

Jean-Michel dies, aged just twenty-seven. In 2016, one of his paintings sells for $110.5 million dollars – the highest amount ever for an American artist.

JEAN-MICHEL BASQUIAT

Mindy Kaling

> **WRITER, COMEDIAN, ACTOR AND PRODUCER-DIRECTOR**
>
> Born – 1979, United States

Little Mindy's parents fell in love in Africa and moved to America before she was born. As a kid, Mindy loved watching movies. When she went to the cinema, she took a notebook with her so she could write down the lines that made her laugh the most. She wanted to make people laugh like that, too! But at the end of every movie, Mindy was always left feeling that she was the only Indian-American girl in the world. At night, she dreamt up all kinds of romantic comedies, written by and starring someone just like her.

When she was grown-up, Mindy wrote funny articles, drew comics, sang and performed comedy – and still found time to graduate as a playwright! Mindy moved to New York and, along with her friend Brenda, wrote a hit play about two famous actors. It won awards and got her noticed by TV companies. She became the only woman writing for a comedy TV show called *The Office*, putting out some of the best dialogue and even starring as a funny character called Kelly Kapoor. The show was a big success and Mindy became a celebrity. But there was so much more she wanted to do.

Mindy began to write bestselling books about her own life, and became the first Indian-American woman to create her own comedy TV show. She starred as Dr Mindy Lahiri, an Indian-American doctor in New York City. Whether she's producing sitcoms, creating comedies, directing shows or writing books, Mindy is doing what she loves most: telling stories. And little Mindy's dream of seeing someone like herself on TV and in films has come true, inspiring a whole new generation of Indian-American girls to think big, break barriers and put themselves where they want to be.

'If you've got it, flaunt it.
And if you don't got it? Flaunt it.'

Mindy Kaling

Vera Mindy Chokalingam is born in Cambridge, Massachusetts. Her family call her 'Mindy'.

At university, Mindy takes theatre classes, is a member of the improv team and writes a popular comic called *Badly Drawn Girl*.

With her friend Brenda Withers, Mindy creates a funny play called *Matt & Ben*, where they pretend to be famous actors Ben Affleck and Matt Damon. It's a big hit.

1979 1987 1998 2001 2002 2004

From an early age, Mindy starts writing – at home, at the cinema, or while waiting for her mother to finish work.

After graduating, Mindy moves to Brooklyn, New York and works as a helper on a TV show, as well as doing stand-up comedy gigs.

Mindy is hired to write and act in TV comedy *The Office*. When she joins, Mindy is only 24 years old and the only woman writer on the show.

The Office is nominated for an Emmy for Outstanding Comedy Series for the fifth year in a row.

The Mindy Project – a TV series written and produced by Mindy, and featuring her in the starring role – is released. It runs for six years.

Praised for breaking Asian stereotypes, Mindy creates the Netflix series *Never Have I Ever*, about an Indian-American girl dealing with the death of her father.

2011 2011 2012 2018 2020 2021

Mindy writes her first memoir, *Is Everyone Hanging Out Without Me (And Other Concerns)*, and then another – *Why Not Me?* – in 2015. Both books are hits, with her second reaching No. 1 on the New York Times bestseller list.

Mindy stars in the all-female version of *Ocean's Eleven*.

Mindy continues to inspire others and make them laugh, working on films and TV series while raising her young family.

Mindy Kaling

Malala Yousafzai

ACTIVIST FOR GIRLS' EDUCATION

Born – 1997, Pakistan

When little Malala was born, her father was determined she would have every opportunity that the world had to offer. Malala knew education was precious, and she couldn't wait to grow up and discover all her talents. Her mother never had the chance to learn how to read and write, but Malala hoped her life would be different. She wanted to prove to everyone that girls can have big dreams, too.

When Malala was ten, a violent group called the Taliban took control of the beautiful valley in Pakistan where she lived. They banned music, television, flying kites, dancing and – most devastating of all – girls going to school. The Taliban thought girls should get married, cover their bodies from head to toe, and never leave the house without their husbands or brothers.

Malala was horrified. Even though she was afraid, she decided to stand up for what she believed in. On television and online, Malala and her friends spoke out against the crime of denying girls an education. For the Taliban, there was nothing scarier than a girl willing to speak up. They shot Malala and two of her friends on the bus home from school, leaving Malala badly injured. When Malala woke up, it was in a hospital in England, far away from home.

But Malala got better... and stronger, and louder. Nothing would stop her from campaigning for a girl's right to education. This time, the whole world listened. She spoke everywhere from the White House to refugee camps, and became the youngest person ever to receive the Nobel Peace Prize. With her father's help, she created a foundation to improve girls' lives and their education. And today Malala continues to fight for children's rights to a future as big and bright as their dreams.

'One child, one teacher, one book and one pen can change the world.'

Malala Yousafzai

Malala is born in Mingora, in an area of Pakistan called Swat Valley.

A violent group called the Taliban take over Swat Valley. They set out new, strict rules and begin closing schools for girls.

Malala is asked to write a diary about her life under Taliban rule for the BBC. She uses the name of a heroine from one of her favourite Pashtun tales, 'Gul Makai'.

1997   2000s   2007   2008   2009   2011

Malala grows up in a happy, loving Muslim family. Her father runs a school for girls, and Malala is a very bright student.

Malala and her friends decide to speak up and share their story on local television. The story spreads all over Pakistan.

Malala begins to win awards for her work, including Pakistan's first National Youth Peace Prize.

When Malala is fifteen, she is shot by the Taliban. Badly injured, she is sent to a hospital in the UK. Children all over the world write her get well cards!

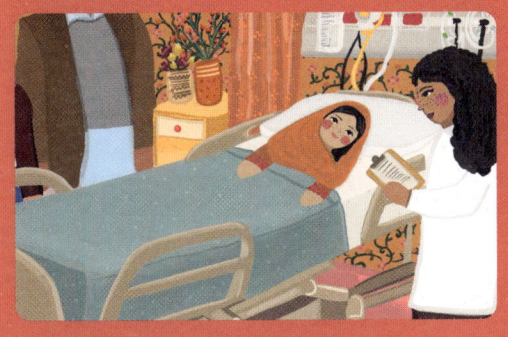

On her sixteenth birthday, Malala speaks in front of the United Nations in New York City. Later that year she visits the White House and meets the president of the USA.

Malala publishes a children's book about her life called *Malala's Magic Pencil*. That same year, she starts studying at Oxford University.

2012 2013 2013 2014 2017 2021

Important people around the world take up Malala's cause. Malala and her father set up the Malala Fund, an organisation that supports girls' education.

Malala shares the Nobel Peace Prize with Kailash Satyarthi, an activist who fights against child labour in India.

After she graduates from university, Malala continues to campaign for the rights of children the world over.

Malala Yousafzai

GRETA THUNBERG

CLIMATE ACTIVIST

Born – 2003, Sweden

Little Greta grew up being kind to nature: she learnt from her parents not to waste water or food, and to turn off the lights. One day at school, she watched a film about climate change, and discovered that human activity was causing the Earth to warm up. Her classmates were worried, but once the film was over, everyone forgot about it. Everyone… except Greta. Greta couldn't understand why more people didn't take climate change seriously. Why was no one in power doing anything to solve this terrible problem?

Greta felt so hopeless about the future that she stopped talking. Doctors said she had selective mutism and Asperger's syndrome, which meant she would only speak and pay attention to what was really important to her. But this ended up being Greta's greatest superpower – it helped her to focus with single-minded determination on her dream: saving the planet.

Greta started by convincing her parents to stop eating meat and taking planes. But she knew she would have to do more. One day, instead of going to school, Greta decided to sit quietly in front of the Swedish Parliament with a sign that read 'School Strike for Climate'. Every Friday she turned up, and each time, more and more students joined her.

Word of Greta's protest spread, and soon thousands of students around the world started skipping school to protest against climate change. Governments were forced to take notice, and Greta crossed the ocean to speak in front of world leaders. She asked them to stop making up excuses and start acting. Inspired by Greta, millions of people from many countries flooded the streets in strikes against global warming – the biggest environmental protest ever! What started with just one girl with a handmade sign and a dream became a global movement that includes us all.

'The moment we decide to fulfil something, we can do anything.'

GRETA THUNBERG

| 2003 | 2014 | 2015 | 2018 | 2018 | 2018 |

2003 — Greta Thunberg is born in Stockholm, Sweden.

2015 — Over the next few years, Greta becomes vegan and persuades her family to stop flying. Here are five planet-saving changes everyone can make:
- Buy less
- Recycle
- Eat less meat
- Avoid plastic
- Fly and drive less; walk and cycle more!

2018 — Other children join Greta's 'School Strike for Climate', first in Sweden, then across the world. Greta travels by train around Europe, joining the strikes.

2014 — Eleven-year-old Greta temporarily stops speaking, and is diagnosed with Asperger's syndrome.

2018 — In August, Greta begins missing school to protest outside the Swedish Parliament.

2018 — In 2018–2019, Greta gives speeches to the United Nations and governments. Her speeches are published in a book called *No One Is Too Small to Make a Difference*.

Inspired by Greta, the first Global Strike for Climate takes place in March. Over a million people in 125 countries take part!

On September 20th, Greta joins protestors in the largest climate change demonstration in history. It involves over four million people in 150 countries.

Greta meets Nobel Prize winner and activist, Malala Yousafzai. Malala says of Greta, 'She's the only friend I'd skip school for.'

2019　2019　2019　2019　2020　2021

In August, sixteen-year-old Greta travels across the Atlantic Ocean on a wind and solar-powered boat to speak at the United Nations Climate Action Summit in New York – the journey takes fifteen days. 'The eyes of all future generations are upon you,' she says, 'And if you choose to fail us, I say – we will never forgive you.'

In December, Greta is named *TIME* magazine's Person of the Year – the youngest person ever to receive the honour.

Greta continues to stand up for the environment, and is seen as a symbol of hope for a cleaner, greener future.

GRETA THUNBERG

The 51st Dreamer

You have now met 50 dreamers and read about their incredible lives – their hopes and fears, their successes and setbacks, and their amazing dreams that helped to make the world a better place. Now, it's time to write about yourself.

1. At the top of a piece of paper, write your name and your date of birth.

2. Try writing the story of your own life. Here are some things to think about.

Who are the people in your life?

What do you like to do?

What are you proud of?

3. Then, draw a portrait of yourself and colour it in.

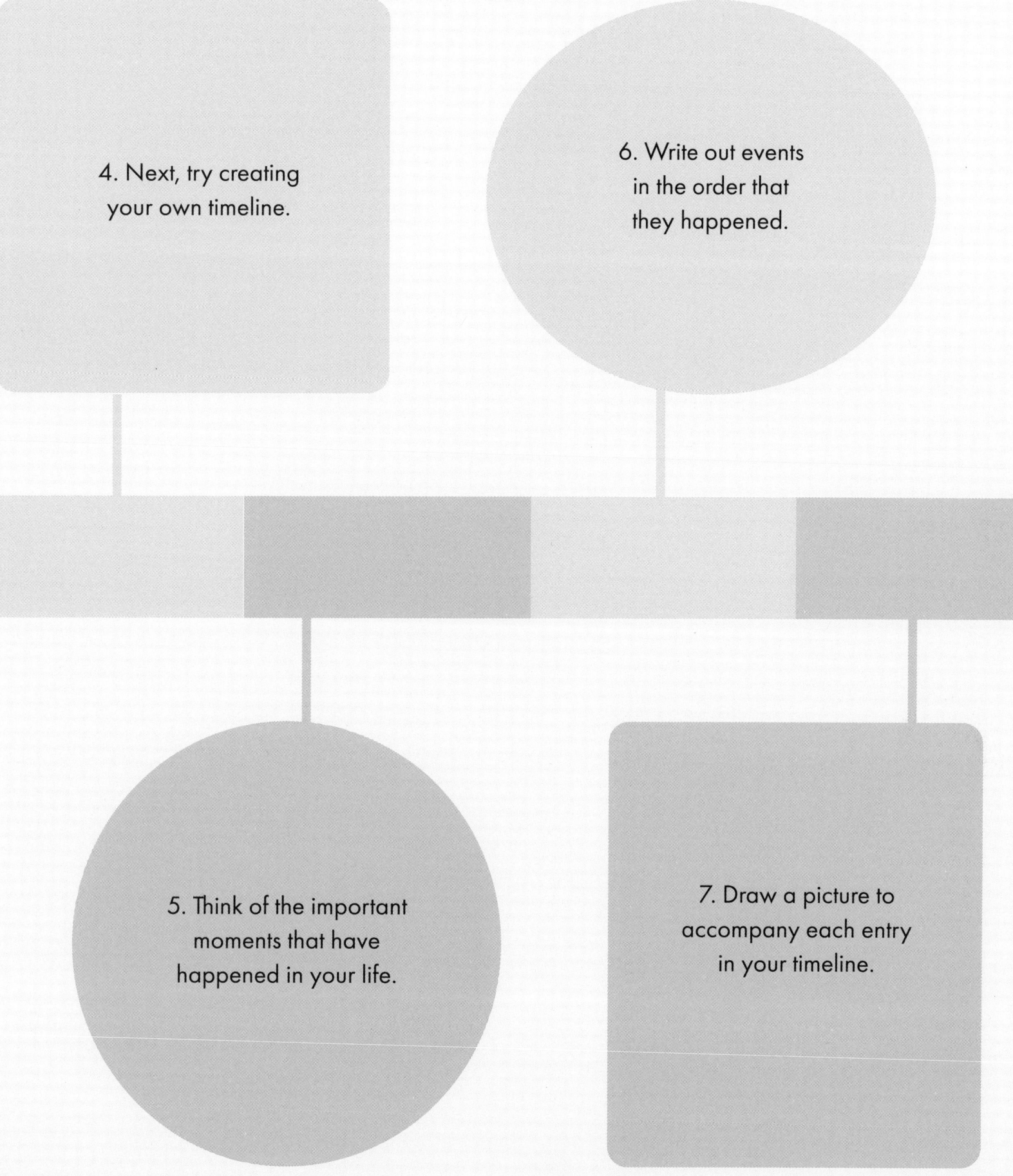

GLOSSARY

Academy Award An annual award recognising achievement in the film industry; also known as an 'Oscar'.

activist A person who takes action to bring about change, for example on issues such as climate change or racism.

alter-ego An alternative personality created by a person.

amateur Someone who does an activity, such as sport, without being paid.

ambassador Someone who represents an organisation or country.

anthropologist Someone who studies human beings in the past and present.

assassinated When someone is killed, often for political reasons.

BBC A British broadcaster.

British Empire A group of countries that in the past were ruled by Britain.

broadcasting The making of television and radio programmes.

choreographer A person who creates dance steps and moves.

circumnavigate To travel all the way around something.

Civil Rights Movement A movement in the United States in the 1950s and 1960s that fought for equal rights for African-Americans.

Civil War (American) The war that was fought between the Southern and Northern states of the United States, from 1981 to 1865. The Southern states wanted to keep slavery, while the Northern states wanted to make it illegal.

climate change A term usually used to describe the process of Earth heating up.

concentration camp A prison camp. In World War Two, the Nazis sent many Jewish and other people to these camps, where they were forced to work or murdered. Many people also died of starvation or disease.

conservation Preserving and protecting the natural world.

couture house A business that designs and sells expensive, fashionable clothing made-to-order for each customer.

cult Something that is very popular or fashionable.

democracy A form of government in which the people have a say in how the country is run.

discrimination The unfair treatment of a particular group of people, for example because of their race or gender.

doctorate One of the highest-ranking degrees given by a university, usually a PhD.

element A solid, liquid or gas that can't be broken down into anything else.

Emmy An annual award recognising achievement in the television industry.

enslavement The practice of owning other people. This was legal in America until 1865; slave owners were allowed to sell people and force them to work without being paid.

feminist Somebody who believes that women and men should have equal rights.

Free State A state in the USA in which slavery did not exist.

gay See LGBTQ+.

Grammy An annual award recognising achievement in the music industry.

Great Depression A period of economic hardship in America and around the world, which lasted from 1929 to 1941. Many banks failed and people lost their jobs, homes and savings.

habitat The natural home of a living thing.

heavyweight The heaviest class of boxers. In the sport, people of similar weights fight each other.

humanitarian A person who works to reduce suffering and make other people's lives better.

inauguration The act or ceremony of welcoming somebody into an important position.

Indigenous The first people to live in a place, for example the Native American people in North America, or the Aboriginal people of Australia.

learning disabilities Difficulties in understanding information or doing everyday activities, which affects someone for their whole life.

LGBTQ+ These letters stand for lesbian, gay, bisexual, transgender, and queer (or questioning) – different forms of sexual or gender identity.

lyrics The words of a song.

malnutrition A health problem in which the body does not get the nutrients it needs.

martial arts Traditional fighting sports from China, Korea or Japan, for example, karate, kung fu and judo.

master mariner A sailor who is qualified to be captain of a merchant ship.

merchant navy A country's ships that carry goods, rather than being used for military activity.

naturalist Someone who studies the natural world.

natural sciences The study of animals and plants in the wild.

Nobel Prize Prestigious annual awards in six areas: physics, chemistry, medicine, literature, peace and economics.

non-violence The use of peaceful protest to bring about change.

occupation The act of a country being overtaken by force.

palaeontologist Someone who studies fossils.

plantation A large farm on which crops such as a sugar, cotton and tobacco are grown.

pop artist An artist from the Pop Art movement of the 1950s and 1960s. The movement was influenced by popular culture such as advertisements and movie stars.

prejudice An unfair opinion about someone formed without any actual knowledge or experience.

Presidential Medal of Freedom The highest award that a civilian (a non-military person) can gain in the United States.

racism The unfair treatment of people because of the colour of their skin or culture.

radiation A type of energy produced by radioactive substances.

reform school A school that young people who have committed a crime are sent to instead of going to prison.

Resistance An organisation that secretly fights against an enemy that has occupied its country.

Rock & Roll Hall of Fame A museum and hall of fame in Cleveland, Ohio, USA, which inducts (admits) a handful of influential musicians and bands every year.

scatting A style of jazz singing using random or nonsense words.

scholarship Money paid to support a student's education.

segregation The practice of keeping people of different races, religions or ethnic groups separate from each other, for example in schools, buses and restaurants.

sexism The unfair treatment of people because of their gender.

slavery See enslavement.

species A group of living things that can breed with each other.

stereotype A fixed idea about what someone or something is like, which is often untrue.

Suffragette Women in the early 20th century who fought to win women the right to vote.

terrorist Someone who uses violence or intimidation to achieve their aims.

United Nations An international organisation that includes almost all the countries in the world. It was set up to promote peace and end wars.

Wimbledon A famous annual international tennis championship, held in London in the UK.

World War One A war that lasted from 1914 to 1918 and involved most of the countries in Europe, as well as Russia, the US, the Middle East and other countries.

World War Two A war that lasted from 1939 to 1945 and was fought between the Allies (Britain, the US, Russia and others) and the Axis (Nazi Germany – led by Adolf Hitler – Japan and Italy).

INDEX

A

Academy Awards 169, 179, 195, 218
activists 6, 7, 16–17, 18–19, 20–21, 22–23, 28–29, 30–31, 49, 62–63, 64–65, 78–79, 80–81, 82–83, 84–85, 95, 96–97, 98–99, 124–125, 126–127, 128–129, 130–131, 134, 137, 142, 154–155, 156–157, 158–159, 160–161, 162–163, 164–165,175, 208–209, 210–211, 212–213, 214–215
actors 90, 104–105, 107, 132, 138–139, 140–141, 166–167, 168–169, 175, 204–205, 206–207
algorithms 15
Ali, Muhammad (Cassius Marcellus Clay Jr) 133, 137, 141, 154–155, 156–157
American Civil Rights Movement 62, 65, 78, 81, 96, 100, 101–102
American Civil War 16, 19
Amundsen, Roald 36, 38
Analytical Engine 15
Angelou, Maya 90, 96–97, 98–99
Anne of Green Gables (book) 40, 43
Antarctica 36, 38–39, 92
Apple (technology company) 77, 188, 191
Aquino, Corazon 91, 112–113, 114–115
Aquino, Benigno ('Ninoy') 112, 114, 115
architects 174, 180–181, 182–183
athletes 49, 82–83, 84–85, 90, 124–125, 126–127, 132, 134–135, 136–137, 138, 140–141, 154–155, 156–157, 162–163, 164–165, 174, 184–185, 186–187
Attenborough, David 90, 92–93, 94–95, 119
Automatic Computing Engine (ACE) 77
aviators 48, 58–59, 60–61

B

Babbage, Charles 12, 14, 15
Baker, Josephine 48, 62–63, 64–65, 110
ballet 104, 106, 120, 122–123, 192, 194
Basquiat, Jean Michel 175, 200–201, 202–203
BBC (British Broadcasting Company) 92, 94, 210, 218
Beatles, The (band) 128, 130, 131
Becquerel, Henri 27
black holes 150, 152
Bletchley Park 76
Bombe (code breaking machine) 74
Bowie, David 132, 170–171, 172–173, 195
boxing 137–138, 140–141, 154, 156–157
broadcasters 90, 92–93, 94–95, 119
Byron, Lord 8, 11, 14

C

calculators 12, 14
Carnegie Hall 65, 89
Chanel, Coco 6, 44–45, 46–47
chemistry 24, 27
Children's House School (Casa dei Bambini) 32, 35
chimpanzees 116, 118, 119
Christie, Agatha 48, 54–55, 56–57
Christie, Archie 56

civil rights 28, 30–31, 48, 62, 65, 78, 80–81, 90, 96, 100–101, 102–103, 158, 161
Civil Rights Act, The 103
Civil Rights Movement (American) 62, 65, 78, 81, 96, 100, 101–102, 158, 161, 218
Civil War (American) 16, 19, 218
climate change activism 92, 95, 142, 145, 174, 212–213, 214–215
code breaking 74–75, 76–77
comedians 204–205
computers 11, 12, 15, 74, 76–77, 150, 153, 180, 188, 190–191
computer programmers 11, 12–13, 14–15
concentration camps 104, 108, 111, 218
conservationists 92–93, 94–95, 116–117, 118–119
Covid-19 169
Curie, Irene 27
Curie, Marie 6, 24–25, 26–27
Curie, Pierre 24, 26

D

dancers 62–63, 64–65, 90, 104–105, 106–107, 120–121, 122–123
diarists 35, 42, 90, 107, 108–11, 210
Diary of Anne Frank, The (book) 108, 111
Diaz, Al 202
Difference Engine 14
Dutch Resistance 104
Dylan, Bob 132, 146–147, 148–149, 191

E

Earhart, Amelia 48, 58–59, 60–61
educators 6, 32–33, 34–35
Elephant Island 36, 39
Emmy Awards 207, 218
Endurance (ship) 36, 38, 39
Enigma code 74
enslavement 16, 18–19
Enter the Dragon (film) 138, 141
Epstein, Brian 130
exotic pets 65, 69
explorers 6, 36–37, 38–39

F

fashion designers 6, 44–45, 46–47, 132, 142–143, 144–145
feminists 8, 20, 218
Fitzgerald, Ella Jane 48, 86–87, 88–89
Flyology (book) 14
Fonteyn, Margot 123
footballers 132, 134–135, 136–137
Football World Cup 134, 137
Foreman, George 157
Formula One 196, 198, 199
Frank, Anne (Annelies) 35, 90, 107, 108–109, 110–11
Frank, Otto 107, 108, 110, 111
Frankenstein (book) 8, 11
Franklin, Aretha Louise 132, 158–159, 160–161

Frazier, Joe 157
French Resistance 62, 65, 110

G

Galapagos Islands 92
Gandhi, Mahatma (Mohandas) 6, 28–29, 30–31, 103
Give Peace a Chance (song) 131
Global Strike for Climate 215
Gombe Stream Research Centre 119
Goodall, Jane 90, 116–117, 118–119
Goodwill Ambassadors 85, 107, 127, 137
Goolagong, Evonne 174, 184–185, 186–187
Goolagong National Development Camp for Indigenous Boys and Girls 187
Grammy Awards 89, 161, 169, 173, 179, 194, 218
Grand Prix 199
Great Depression, USA 88, 218

H

Hadid, Zaha 174, 180–181, 182–183
Hans Christian Anderson medal 73
Harriet Tubman Home for the Aged, The 19
Hawks, Frank 60
Hawking Radiation 152
Hawking, Stephen 132, 150–151, 152–153
Henry Ford Museum, Detroit 81
Hepburn, Audrey 90, 104–105, 106–107
Hollywood 107, 138, 141
Howland Island 61
humanitarians 104–105, 106–107

I

I have a dream (speech) 100, 103
I Know Why the Caged Bird Sings (book) 96
Imagine (song) 128
Indian independence 31
industrial revolution 8, 10
International Congress for Women 34
inventors 48, 74–75, 76–77, 174, 188–189, 190–191
iPhone 77, 191

J

Jane Goodall Foundation 119
jazz 48, 49, 86, 88–89, 170, 192, 194
Jeet Kune Do 138, 141
Jobs, Steve 77, 174, 188–189, 190–191
John, Elton 131, 174, 176–177, 178–179

K

Kahlo, Frida 48, 66–67, 68–69
Kaling, Mindy 174, 204–205, 206–207
King, Billie Jean 132, 162–163, 164–165, 179, 186
King Edward Island 40, 42–43
King Jr, Martin Luther 65, 81, 89, 90, 96, 98, 100–103, 161
King, William (Earl of Lovelace) 15
Kirov Ballet 120, 122
kung fu 138, 140

L

Leakey, Dr Louis 116, 118
Lee, Bruce 132, 138–139, 140–141, 157
Lennon, John 90, 128–129, 130–131, 173
LGBTQ+ rights 77, 165, 179
Life on Earth (TV show) 95, 119
Lifetime Achievement Award 173
Lindgren, Astrid 43, 48, 70–71, 72–73
Lindgren, Karin 70, 72–73
Lindgren, Sture 72
Liston, Sonny 154, 156
Little Curies (Petites Curies) 27
Living Legend Award 85
Longstocking, Pippi 43, 70, 72–73
Lovelace, Ada 6, 11, 12–13, 14–15

M

Malala's Magic Pencil (book) 211
Malcom X 96, 98
Man, Master Yip 140
Marcos, Ferdinand 112, 114–115
martial arts 132, 138–141, 154, 157
mathematicians 6, 12–13, 14–15, 48, 74–75, 76–77
McLaren, Malcolm 142, 144
Miss Marple 54, 57
monkeys 69, 70, 92
Montessori, Maria 6, 32–33, 34–35
Montgomery Bus Boycott 78, 81, 100, 102
Montgomery, Lucy Maud 6, 40–41, 42–43
Morcom, Christopher 74, 76
motor neuron disease (MND) 152
Mousetrap, The (play) 57
Murder at the Vicarage (book) 57
Murder on the Orient Express (book) 57

N

NAACP (National Association for the Advancement of Colored People) 80
National Youth Peace Prize 210
naturalists 90, 92–95
Nimrod (ship) 38
Ninety nines 61
Nobel prizes
- Literature 146, 149
- Peace Prize 103, 208, 211
- Science (Physics and Chemistry) 24, 27

Noonan, Fred 61
Nureyev, Rudolph 90, 120–121, 122–123

O

Office, The (TV show) 204, 206–207
O'Keeffe, Georgia 48, 50–51, 52–53, 68
Olympics 82, 84–85, 124, 126–127, 154, 156
Ono, Yoko 128, 131
Order of the British Empire 145, 153, 183
Oscar Awards 107
Owens, Jesse 48, 82–83, 84–85, 127
Owl, Grey 94

P

painters 48, 50–51, 52–53 66–67, 68–69, 174, 200–201, 202–203
Pankhurst, Emmeline 6, 20–21, 22–23, 60
Pankhurst, Richard 20

Parks, Raymond 78, 80
Parks, Rosa 19, 48, 78–79, 80–81, 100
Parton, Dolly 132, 166–167, 168–169
Patterson, Floyd 156
Pelé 132, 134–135, 136–137
performers 48, 62–63, 64–65, 86–87, 88–89
Pfeffer, Fritz 111
Philippe Chatrier Award 187
physics 24, 26, 27, 152
physicists 132, 150–151, 152–153
Pixar 191
planet 3204 Lindgren 70
Planet Earth (TV show) 95
Poirot, Hercule 54, 56, 57
polio 68, 124, 126
politicians 6, 28–29, 30–31, 90, 112–113, 114–115
polonium 24, 26
Presidential Medal of Freedom (USA) 81, 82, 85, 89, 99, 149, 153, 157, 165
primatologists 90, 116–117, 118–119
Prince (Prince Rogers Nelson) 174, 192–193, 194–195
Pritzker prize 183
protest 20, 23, 28, 30–31, 100, 102–103, 128, 131, 142, 145, 148, 154, 157, 165, 212, 214
Prost, Alain 196
punk 142, 144
Purple Rain (film and album) 195

Q

Queen Elizabeth II 57, 92, 95, 128, 131, 145, 179, 183

R

racing drivers 174, 196–197, 198–199
racism 62, 78, 80, 82, 85, 96, 100, 200
radiation 27, 152
radioactivity 24
radium 24–27
Radium Institute 27
rainbow tribe 65
Resistance (World War Two) 62, 65, 100, 219
Rhee, Jhoon 157
Riggs, Bobby 162, 165
Riley, Charles 84
Rivera, Diego 66, 68
Rock and Roll Hall of Fame 149, 158, 161, 179
Royal Academy of Music, London 176, 178
Rudolph, Wilma 90, 124–125, 126–127

S

satyagraha 30
scatting 89
scientists 6, 24–25, 26–27, 132, 150–151, 152–153
Scottsboro Boys 80
seamstress 44, 46
segregation 62, 78, 81, 82, 84, 86, 100, 102–103, 126, 127
Senna, Ayrton 174, 196–197, 198–199
Shackleton, Ernest Henry 6, 36–37, 38–39
Shelley, Mary 6, 8–9, 10–11
Shelley, Percy Bysshe 8, 10
singer–songwriters 44, 46, 48, 86, 88–89, 90, 128–129, 130–131, 132, 146–147, 148–149, 158–159, 160–161, 166–167, 168–169, 170–171, 172–173, 174, 176–177, 178–179, 192–193, 194–195
slavery 16, 18–19, 78

Southern Christian Leadership Conference SCLC 102
spies 62, 65, 110
Stardust, Ziggy 170, 173
Stieglitz, Alfred 50, 52
suffrage 20–23
suffragettes 19–20, 23
surfing 56

T

Taliban 208, 210–211
tennis 132, 162–163, 164–165, 174, 184–185, 186–187
Thunberg, Greta 95, 175, 212–213, 214–215
TIME Magazine 47, 115, 137, 215
Toleman Team 199
Tubman, Harriet 6, 16–17, 18–19
Turing, Alan Mathison 15, 48, 74–75, 76–77
Turing test 77
Two Fridas, The (painting) 69

U

Underground Railroad 16, 18
UNESCO (United Nations Educational, Scientific and Cultural Organisation) 137
UNICEF (United Nations Children Fund) 104, 107, 137
United Nations, 119, 137, 211, 214, 215

V

Van Pels, Peter 111
Villekulla 70
Voting Rights Act, The 103

W

Wagoner, Porter 166, 168
Walker, Clyde 164
Warhol, Andy 203
Webb, Chick 86, 88
Westwood, Vivienne 47, 132, 142–143, 144–145
Wildlife on One (TV show) 92
Wimbledon 164, 184, 186, 187
Wing Chun 138, 141
Wollstonecraft, Mary 10
women's rights 8, 20, 60, 158, 160, 162, 165
writers 6, 7, 8–9, 10–11, 40–41, 42–43 48, 54–55, 56–57, 70–71, 72–73, 90, 96–97, 98–99, 175, 204–205, 206–207
Women's Tennis Association 162, 165
World War One 20, 27, 39, 54, 56
World War Two 47, 62, 65, 74, 76, 104, 106, 108, 110, 128, 130, 144
Wozniak, Steve 188, 190, 191

X

X-ray machine 27

Y

Yousafzai, Malala 174, 208–209, 210–211, 215

Z

zoology 92
Zoo Quest (TV show) 94

CREDITS

Miniature of Mary Shelley painted posthumously, after 1822 © The Bodleian Library, University of Oxford, Shelley relics (d); Mary Shelley: Portrait of Mary Shelley by Richard Rothwell drawn in 1840 © GL Archive / Alamy Stock Photo;

Ada Lovelace: Young Ada Lovelace, 1819 © Science History Images / Alamy Stock Photo; Ada Lovelace, aged seventeen, 1832 © GL Archive / Alamy Stock Photo; Ada Lovelace portrait c. 1840 © ART Collection / Alamy Stock Photo

Harriet Tubman: Harriet Tubman, 1868–1869 from the Collection of the Smithsonian National Museum of African American History and Culture shared with the Library of Congress; Harriet Tubman (nee Araminta Ross; c.1822–1913), born into slavery, was an American abolitionist, humanitarian, and an armed scout and spy for the United States Army during the American Civil War. Portrait by Horatio Seymour Squyer c. 1885 © IanDagnall Computing / Alamy Stock Photo; Harriet Tubman (c. 1822–1913). Portrait of the American abolitionist and former slave, c. 1911 © IanDagnall Computing / Alamy Stock Photo

Emmeline Pankhurst: The militant campaigner for female suffrage Emmeline Pankhurst (c) and one of her daughters are welcomed to a meeting of fellow suffragettes with banners and flowers. 1908 © Hulton Deutsch / Contributor via Getty Images; Members of the Pankhurst family who campaigned for women to have the vote in Britain 1917 © Universal History Archive / Contributor via Getty Images; Mrs. Emmeline Pankhurst, addressing crowd of five thousand on historic Boston Common. 1918 © Bettmann / Contributor via Getty Images

Marie Curie: Marie Curie as a child with her brother and sisters. From left to right are Zosia, Hela, Manya (Marie Curie), Joseph and Bronya © Lebrecht Music & Arts / Alamy Stock Photo; Marie and Pierre Curie, 1895 © IanDagnall Computing / Alamy Stock Photo; 1906: Marie Curie, French physicist and winner of the 1903 Nobel Prize for Physics, which she shared with her husband Pierre Curie. She was the first woman to win a Nobel Prize © Hulton Archive / Stringer via Getty Images; Marie Curie, Polish-born French physicist, with her daughter Irene Joliot-Curie, 1925 © Oxford Science Archive/ Print Collector / Contributor via Getty Images

Gandhi: Gandhi, Mahatma, 1876 © ullstein bild Dtl. / Contributor via Getty Images; 1888. Nineteen-year-old Gandhi sets sail to London to study law © History and Art Collection / Alamy Stock Photo; Gandhi, Mohandas Karamchand Gandhi (1869–1948) Indian lawyer and anti-colonial nationalist © GL Archive / Alamy Stock Photo; Leader of India, Mohandas Gandhi. 1 November, 1942 © Wallace Kirkland / Contributor via Getty Images

Maria Montessori: 1880 – Maria Montessori age 10, 1880 © The Maria Montessori Archives held at Association Montessori Internationale, Amsterdam; Maria Montessori and child in the classroom © ullstein bild Dtl. / Contributor via Getty Images; Maria Montessori, c. 1930 © ullstein bild Dtl. / Contributor via Getty Images

Ernest Shackleton: Vintage photo circa 1910s of British Antarctic explorer Sir Ernest Henry Shackleton (1874–1922) © Archive Pics / Alamy Stock Photo; Sir Ernest Shackleton setting out on his heroic journey of 750 miles from Elephant Island to South Georgia in a small boat, the 'James Caird', to seek help for his comrades © PA Images / Alamy Stock Photo; Ernest Shackleton Posing in His Officer Uniform © George Rinhart / Contributor via Getty Images

L. M. Montgomery: L. M. Montgomery age 9 © L. M. Montgomery Collection, University of Guelph – 1883; L. M. Montgomery age 14 © L. M. Montgomery Collection, University of Guelph – 1888; L. M. Montgomery frontispiece of diary, age 28 © L. M. Montgomery Collection, University of Guelph – 1902; L. M. Montgomery age 61, 1935 © L. M. Montgomery Collection, University of Guelph – 1935

Coco Chanel: GABRIELLE 'COCO' CHANEL (1883–1971). French fashion designer. Photographed on the beach in Etretat, Normandy, early 20th century © Granger Historical Picture Archive / Alamy Stock Photo; Gabrielle Chanel, known as Coco (1883–1971), top French couturier, at Faubourg, St Honore, Paris © Hulton Deutsch / Contributor via Getty Images; Coco Chanel, 1954 © Everett Collection Historical / Alamy Stock Photo

Artist Georgia O'Keeffe stands next to her painting Horse Skull with White Rose at an exhibit of her work titled Life and Death © Bettmann / Contributor via Getty Images; American artist Georgia O'Keeffe (1887–1986) on a morning walk around Ghost Ranch, Abiquiu, New Mexico, 1966 © John Loengard / Contributor via Getty Images

Agatha Christie: Agatha Christie as a young girl, c. 1900 © The Christie Archive Trust; Agatha Christie, who has mysteriously disappeared in England, 1926 © Bettmann / Contributor via Getty Images; English detective novelist, Agatha Christie (1890–1976) typing at her home, Greenway House, Devon, January 1946 © Bettmann / Contributor via Getty Images; Writer Agatha Christie with Queen Elizabeth at the premiere of the film "Murder on the Orient Express", London (England), 26 November 1974 © Farabola / Alamy Stock Photo

Amelia Earhart: American aviator Amelia Earhart (1897–1937) as young girl, 1904 © FPG / Staff; Pilot Amelia Earhart poses for a portrait in c. 1928 © Donaldson Collection / Contributor via Getty Images; Arrival of Amelia Earhart in Derry after her solo transatlantic flight, May 20, 1932, in Northern Ireland, United Kingdom © API / Contributor via Getty Images

Josephine Baker: American born singer and dancer Josephine Baker (1906–1975), surrounded by male dancers at the Bergere © Topical Press Agency / Stringer via Getty Images; Josephine Baker, La Folie Du Jour revue at Folies-Bergere, Paris, 1926 © Glasshouse Images / Alamy Stock Photo; Josephine Baker, 1 January, 1970 © Michael Ochs Archives / Stringer via Getty Images; Josephine Baker in the uniform of the 'Cevalier of the Legion of Honour' – about 1945 © ullstein bild Dtl. / Contributor via Getty Images

Frida Kahlo: Frida Kahlo as a young girl, 1919 © FineArt / Alamy Stock Photo; Photo shows Mrs. Diego Rivera painting one now, and she is doing a mural for the San Francisco Stock Exchange, with one of her portraits of a San Francisco society woman © Bettmann / Contributor via Getty Images; 1944: Photograph of Frida Kahlo (1910–1954), Mexican painter, holding a monkey © Bettmann / Contributor via Getty Images; Artist Frida Rivera Three Times. Spectacular sample of the distinctive art of Frida Kahlo Rivera, is this painting entitled, Me Twice. The artist stands at left. Painting shows the artist as a 19th Century lady, left, linked by blood vessels to the artist conceived as an Indian. October 24, 1939 © Bettmann / Contributor via Getty Images

Astrid Lindgren: Astrid Lindgren, Swedish author 1987 © Roger Tillberg / Alamy Stock Photo

1930 – Alan Turing, c. 1930s © Heritage Images / Contributor via Getty Images; Electronic engineer Edward Newman Pilot Model ACE, designed by Alan Turing, 1950 © Jimmy Sime / Stringer via Getty Images

Rosa Parks: A photograph of the childhood home of Rosa Parks that is part of a Rosa Parks archive 1919 © The Washington Post / Contributor via Getty Images; Rosa Parks Mug Shot 1955. Arrested for refusing to relinquish her seat on a bus in Montgomery, Alabama © Photo 12 / Contributor via Getty Images; American civil rights activist, Rosa Parks sits in the front of a bus in Montgomery, Alabama, after the Supreme Court ruled segregation illegal on the city bus system on December 21st, 1956 © Bettmann / Contributor via Getty Images; Rosa Parks receives the Presidential Medal of Freedom from President Bill Clinton, Sept. 14, 1996 © Everett Collection Inc / Alamy Stock Photo; MSX International employee Jeff Doran washes the historic Montgomery, Alabama, bus No. 2857, on which Rosa Parks refused to give up her seat to a white man on December 1, 1955 (2003) © Sipa US / Alamy Stock Photo

Jesse Owens: 13th June 1932: American track athlete Jesse Owens (1913–1980) smiles just after he broke the world record for the 100 meter dash as a high school student, Cleveland, Ohio © New York Times Co. / Contributor via Getty Images; American Sprinter Jesse Owens Pumping Gas At A Gas Station In Cleveland On August 1, 1935 © Keystone-France / Contributor via Getty Images; Jesse Owens at the start of the 200 metres at the 1936 Berlin Olympics which he won in 20.7 seconds, an Olympic record, 1936 ©Print Collector / Contributor via Getty Images; Athletes watch as Jesse Owens coaches them during his 1955 goodwill trip to India © James Burke / Contributor via Getty Images

Ella Fitzgerald: Ella Fitzgerald, portrait ca. 1930s © Everett Collection Inc / Alamy Stock Photo; 1938: American jazz singer Ella Fitzgerald sings while holding sheet music on stage with American bandleader Chick Webb, as an audience looks on, Asbury Park Casino, Asbury Park, New Jersey © Hulton Archive / Stringer via Getty Images; Ella Fitzgerald performs before a packed house at Roy Thomson Hall © Mike Slaughter / Contributor via Getty Images

David Attenborough: England, 1956, A portrait of British naturalist and broadcaster David Attenborough © Popperfoto / Contributor via Getty Images; David Attenborough – Personalities. June 18, 1971 © Fairfax Media Archives / Contributor via Getty Images; Sir David Attenborough during a photo opportunity at Taronga Park Zoo October 13, 2003 in Sydney, Australia © Daniel Berehulak/Getty Images.

Maya Angelou: Maya Angelou (b. 1928), began her career as a dancer and writer. 1957 portrait dressed for her part in the Caribbean Calypso Festival © Everett Collection Inc / Alamy Stock Photo; CREATIVITY WITH BILL MOYERS, guest Maya Angelou, PBS-TV, 1982 © Everett Collection Inc / Alamy Stock Photo; American poet Maya Angelou reciting her poem 'On the Pulse of Morning' at the inauguration of President Bill Clinton in Washington DC, 20th January 1993 © Consolidated News Pictures / Contributor via Getty Images; U.S. President Barack Obama presents poet and author Maya Angelou with the 2010 Medal of Freedom in the East Room of the White House February 15, 2011 in Washington, DC © Chip Somodevilla / Staff via Getty Images

Martin Luther King Jr.: The Afro-American politician and leader for the civil rights movement MARTIN LUTHER KING Jr (1929–1968) aged 19 at Atlanta Baptist College, the day of his graduation in Sociology © ARCHIVIO GBB / Alamy Stock Photo; In this handout, American Baptist minister and activist Martin Luther King Jr (1929–1968) in a mug shot following his arrest during the Montgomery bus boycotts, Alabama, US, February 1956 © Kypros/Getty Images; American Civil Rights leader Dr. Martin Luther King Jr. (1929–1968) addresses the crowd at the March On Washington D.C., 28th August 1963 © CNP/Getty Images; Dr. Martin Luther King, Jr. arrives in Montgomery, Alabama on March 25th 1965 at the culmination of the Selma to Montgomery March. Pictured from left, Ralph Bunche, Dr. Martin Luther King, Jr., Coretta Scott King, Rev. Fred Shuttlesworth, Hosea Williams © Morton Broffman / Contributor via Getty Images

Audrey Hepburn: Audrey Hepburn places her name on the top of the theater's marquee. The Belgian-born actress, who was appearing on Broadway for the first time, scored in the title role of a new version of the perennial comedy, Gigi © Bettmann / Contributor via Getty Images; Audrey Hepburn holding the Academy Award for best actress in Roman Holiday, her first American film © Bettmann / Contributor via Getty Images; British actress and humanitarian Audrey Hepburn (1929–1993) with an Ethiopian girl on her first field mission for UNICEF in Ethiopia, 16th-17th March 1988 © Derek Hudson / Contributor via Getty Images

Anne Frank: Anne Frank (1929–1945) in 1935, taken from her photo album ©

Anne Frank Fonds Basel / Contributor via Getty Images; Two pages from the diary of Anne Frank, written during her years in hiding during World War II, c. 1942 © Anne Frank Fonds Basel / Contributor via Getty Images; Anne Frank, 1942, Photo Collection Anne Frank House, Amsterdam, Public Domain Work

Corazon Aquino: 1940 – Young Corazon. Shared with permission from the Aquino family; 1979 – Corazon Aquino poses with her family. Shared with permission from the Aquino family; Corazon Aquino, 52, widow of murdered opposition leader Benigno Aquino, flashes the Laban (fight) sign before thousands of supporters who jammed a public plaza in Tarlac in December 17, 1985 © REUTERS / Alamy Stock Photo; Corazon (Cory) Aquino attends a rally prior to the so-called 'snap' elections © Peter Charlesworth / Contributor via Getty Images

Jane Goodall: Jane Goodall, c. 1965 © Everett Collection Historical / Alamy Stock Photo; Jane Goodall, English primatologist, ethologist, and anthropologist, with a chimpanzee in her arms, c. 1995 © Apic / Contributor via Getty Images; British environmentalist Jane Goodall poses for a portrait at the garden of Groningen University at the Sharing the Planet conference June 14, 2002 in Groningen, Netherlands © Michel Porro / Stringer via Getty Images

Rudolf Nureyev: Young dancer Nureyev during exercise at the barre, c. 1950s © AGIP / Bridgeman Images; Margot Fonteyn and partner Rudolf Nureyev in the ballet, 'Pelleas et Melisande.' © Keystone Press / Alamy Stock Photo; Rudolf Nureyev 1883 © Time & Life Pictures / Contributor via Getty Images

Wilma Rudolph: Wilma Rudolph of the United States, track & field athlete, looks on in a photo dated July 1959 © Robert Riger / Contributor via Getty Images; USA Wilma Rudolph, 1960 Summer Olympics © Mark Kauffman / Contributor via Getty Images; Olympic Gold Medal Winner Wilma Rudolph Graduating from College © Bettmann / Contributor via Getty Images; Athlete Wilma Rudolph attends U.S. Olympic Team Benefit Party on October 27, 1978 at the New York Stock Exchange in New York City © Ron Galella / Contributor via Getty Images

John Lennon: Headshot portrait of British musician and songwriter John Lennon (1940 –1980), of the pop group The Beatles, as a young boy in a school uniform and cap, c. 1948 © Hulton Archive / Staff via Getty Images; Singer and guitarist John Lennon before the formation of The Beatles, c. 1959 © Michael Ochs Archives / Stringer via Getty Images; 1963. The phenomenon that was the Beatles. Left to Right: Ringo Starr on drums, George Harrison on guitar, Paul McCartney on bass and vocals, and John Lennon on acoustic guitars and vocals © Bob Thomas / Contributor via Getty Images

Pelé: Brazil's young international star Pele, portrait, 1958 © Popperfoto via Getty Images; Pelé's Overhead Kick, 1965 © Popperfoto via Getty Images; Brazilian soccer legend Pele is in Paris for a friendly match but today he appears in front of the Eiffel Tower, holding the FIFA World Cup trophy. The Jules Rimet Trophy went to Brazil after the team's third victory in this event in 1970 © Universal/Corbis/VCG via Getty Images; Former soccer player Pelé, in Rio de Janeiro, Brazil, 1991 © Paulo Fridman/Corbis via Getty Images

Bruce Lee: Chinese American actor Bruce Lee (1940–1973), in the television series 'The Green Hornet', mid 1960s © Archive Photos/Getty Images; Photo of Bruce Lee in a scene from 'The Big Boss,' 1971 © Michael Ochs Archives/Getty Images;

Vivienne Westwood: Vivienne Westwood, 1977 © Peter Cade via Getty Images; British fashion designer Vivienne Westwood acknowledges applause from the public at the end of the presentation of her Spring/Summer 2008 ready-to-wear collection in Paris, October 1, 2007 © UPI Photo/Eco Clement; Fashion Designer Vivienne Westwood speaks in support as anti-fracking demonstrators stage a protest in London to co-incide with the Shale Gas Forum, a commercial fracking industry event © Patricia Phillips/Alamy Live News

Bob Dylan: Bob Dylan recording in the studio with his acoustic guitar and an assortment of harmonicas in 1961 or 1962 © Michael Ochs Archives/Getty Images; Folk singers Joan Baez and Bob Dylan perform during a civil rights rally on August 28, 1963 in Washington D.C. © Rowland Scherman/National Archive/Newsmakers; Bob Dylan plays a Fender Stratocaster electric guitar for the first time on stage as he performs at the Newport Folk Festival on July 25, 1965 in Newport, Rhode Island © Alice Ochs/Michael Ochs Archives/Getty Images; US President Barack Obama presents the Presidential Medal of Freedom to musician Bob Dylan during a ceremony on May 29, 2012 in the East Room of the White House in Washington. The award is the country's highest civilian honor © MANDEL NGAN/AFP/GettyImages

Stephen Hawking: Cosmologist Stephen Hawking on October 10, 1979 in Princeton, New Jersey © Santi Visalli/Getty Images; Dr Stephen Hawking Physics professor and author at Cambridge University. 1st September 1988 © Brian Randle/Mirrorpix/Getty Images

Muhammad Ali: At 12-years old Cassius Clay (later Muhammad Ali) shows his best pugilist stance. 1954 © Bettmann / Contributor via Getty Images; Heavyweight champion Muhammad Ali stands over Sonny Liston and taunts him to get up during their title fight, 1965 © Bettmann / Contributor via Getty Images; U.S. President George W. Bush (R) awards boxing legend Muhammad Ali (C) with the Presidential Medal of Freedom, as Ali's wife Lonnie watches, during a ceremony in the East Room of the White House in Washington November 9, 2005 © Brooks Kraft LLC/Corbis via Getty Images

Aretha Franklin: Musician Aretha Franklin recording at the piano at Columbia Studios in 1962 in New York © Donaldson Collection/Michael Ochs Archives/Getty Images; Singer Aretha Franklin and producer Jerry Wexler receive their gold records for their hit single 'I Never Loved A Man (The Way I Love You)' in 1967 in New York City, New York © Michael Ochs Archives/Getty Images; Opera singer Luciano Pavarotti (R) laughs along with singer Aretha Franklin (L) and the group Boyz II Men (rear) after accepting the eighth MusiCares Foundation "Person of the Year" award in New York, 23 February, 1998 © HENNY RAY ABRAMS/AFP via Getty Images; Aretha Franklin sings during the inauguration of Barack Obama as the 44th President of the United States of America on the West Front of the Capitol January 20, 2009 in Washington, D.C. © Alex Wong/Getty Images

Billie Jean King: 2nd July 1966: American tennis player Billie-Jean King lifts the trophy above her head after beating Brazil's Maria Bueno to win the women's singles title at the Wimbledon Lawn Tennis Championships © Keystone/Getty Images; Billie Jean King at the Forest Hills Tennis Stadium circa 1973 in Forest Hills, Queens © PL Gould/IMAGES/Getty Image; President Barack Obama (R) embraces tennis champion Billie Jean King after presenting her with the Medal of Freedom during a ceremony in the East Room of the White House August 12, 2009 in Washington, D.C. © Chip Somodevilla/Getty Image

Dolly Parton: Country singer Dolly Parton poses for a portrait in circa 1955 in Tennessee. © Michael Ochs Archives/Getty Images; Country singer Dolly Parton performs onstage with an acoustic guitar in circa 1974 © Michael Ochs Archives/Getty Images; Dolly Parton sighted on location filming Nine to Five on March 18, 1980 in Beverly Hills, California © Ron Galella, Ltd./Ron Galella Collection via Getty Images; Dolly Parton, 1987 © The LIFE Picture Collection via Getty Images

David Bowie: English singer-songwriter and actor David Bowie (then known as Davie or Davy Jones) poses for a portrait at home circa 1966 in London, England © Cyrus Andrews/Michael Ochs Archives/Getty Images; David Bowie (1947–2016) performs on stage on his Ziggy Stardust/Aladdin Sane tour in London, 1973 © Michael Putland/Getty Images; David Bowie poses for a portrait in 1976 © Michael Ochs Archives/Getty Images; Labyrinth (1986) – David Bowie © Moviestore Collection Ltd / Alamy Stock Photo

Elton John: Singer and composer Elton John poses for a portrait shoot in the South of France © Hamish Brown/Contour by Getty Images; James Lomas, George Maguire and Liam Mower with Elton John perform the finale of the Opening Night and World Premiere of "Billy Elliot: The Musical" at the Victoria Palace Theatre on May 12, 2005 in London © Gareth Davies/Getty Images

Zaha Hadid: Iraqi architect Zaha Hadid in her London office, UK, circa 1985 © Christopher Pillitz/Getty Images; Azerbaijan, Baku, Heydar Aliyev cultural center futuristic monument designed by the architect Zaha Hadid, photographed in 2014 © Hemis / Alamy Stock Photo

Evonne Goolagong: Tennis pro Evonne Goolagong with racket, 1960 © Keystone Press/ Alamy Stock Photo; International Tennis Championships at Hilversum, Evonne Goolagong (winner) with Cup, 1971 © BNA Photographic / Alamy Stock Photo; Australia coach Yvonne Cawley and Nicole Pratt of Australia during her defeat to Justine Henin of Belgium at the Prince Leopold Tennis Club, Brussels in Belgium, 2002 © Mike Hewitt/Getty Images; Australia Day Honours List recipient Evonne Goolagong Cawley poses for a photo with her Companion in the General Division of the Order of Australia (AC) award on day 13 of the 2018 Australian Open at Melbourne Park on January 27, 2018 in Melbourne, Australia © Quinn Rooney/Getty Images

Steve Jobs: The celebrated Steve Jobs (Steven Paul, 1955–2011) when he was a young man aged 17. Unknown photographer. Via Alamy Stock Photo; Jobs & Wozniak At The West Coast Computer Faire, 1977 © Tom Munnecke/Getty Images; Steven Jobs, confounder of Apple Computer, who left the company © Mark Kauffman/The LIFE Images Collection via Getty Images/Getty Images; Apple CEO Steve Jobs is pictured giving his Keynote address at Apple Computer's 2006 WWDC in San Francisco August 7, 2006 © Kim Kulish/Corbis via Getty Images

Prince: Singer song-writer and musician Prince performs at the Roxy Theatre on November 26, 1979 in Los Angeles (now in West Hollywood), California © Sherry Rayn Barnett / Michael Ochs Archives/Getty Images; American singer, songwriter and musician Prince, circa 1985 © The LIFE Picture Collection via Getty Images; Prince performs during the "Pepsi Halftime Show" at Super Bowl XLI between the Indianapolis Colts and the Chicago Bears on February 4, 2007 at Dolphin Stadium in Miami Gardens, Florida © Jonathan Daniel/Getty Images

Ayrton Senna: Ayrton Senna, c. 1960s © Sipa/Shutterstock; Ayrton Senna, Toleman-Hart TG184, Grand Prix of France, Dijon-Prenois, 20 May 1984 © Paul-Henri Cahier/Getty Images; Ayrton Senna At Silverstone © 1983 Bob Thomas Sports Photography via Getty Images; Ayrton Senna of Brazil, driver of the #12 John Player Special Team Lotus Lotus 97T Renault V6, turbo celebrates winning his first Grand Prix at the Portuguese Grand Prix on 21st April 1985 at the Autodromo do Estoril in Estoril, Portugal © Grand Prix Photo/Getty Images

Jean-Michel Basquiat: American artist Jean-Michel Basquiat (1960–1988), New York, 1985 © Evelyn Hofer/Getty Images; Untitled, a painting by Jean-Michel Basquiat from 1982, is on display at a media preview for Sotheby's New York evening auctions of Impressionist & Modern Art (16 May) and Contemporary Art (18 May) at Sotheby's in New York City on May 5, 2017 © John Angelillo/UPI/Alamy Stock Photo

Mindy Kaling: Mindy Kaling in 'Is That All There Is?', The Mindy Project, Season 6, Episode 1, aired September 12, 2017 © Jordin Althaus/Hulu/ courtesy Everett Collection; Cate Blanchett, Awkwafina, Sarah Paulson, Anne Hathaway, Sandra Bullock, Mindy Kaling, Helena Bonham Carter and Rihanna attend the Ocean's 8 World Premiere at Alice Tully Hall on June 5, 2018 in New York City © Jamie McCarthy/Getty Images; Mindy Kaling attends the 2020 Vanity Fair Oscar Party hosted by Radhika Jones at Wallis Annenberg Center for the Performing Arts on February 09, 2020 in Beverly Hills, California © Rich Fury/VF20/Getty Images for Vanity Fair

Malala Yousafzai: Malala Yousafzai, 12, lives in the Swat Valley with her family, pictured on March 26, 2009 © Veronique de Viguerie/Getty Images; Pakistani student Malala Yousafzai speaks to the media at UN headquarters in New York, 2013 © STAN HONDA/AFP via Getty Images; Nobel laureate Malala Yousafzai speaks during an exclusive interview with Reuters in Maiduguri, Nigeria July 18, 2017 © Reuters/Afolabi Sotunde/Alamy Stock Photo

Greta Thunberg: Greta Thunberg leads a school strike and sits outside of Riksdagen, the Swedish parliament building for climate change on August 28, 2018 in Stockholm © Jasper Chamber / Alamy Stock Photo; 15-year-old Swedish climate activist Greta Thunberg at COP 24, the 24th Conference of the Parties to the United Nations Framework Convention on Climate Change. Katowice, Poland on 5 December, 2018 © Beata Zawrzel/NurPhoto via Getty Images; Teenage Swedish climate activist Greta Thunberg delivers brief remarks surrounded by other student environmental advocates during a strike to demand action be taken on climate change outside the White House on September 13, 2019 in Washington, DC © Sarah Silbiger/Getty Images; Greta Thunberg attends Fridays For Future Strike on December 13, 2019 in Turin, Italy © Giorgio Perottino/Getty Images

Emmeline Pankhurst, Rosa Parks and Maya Angelou text © 2021 Lisbeth Kaiser.
All other text © 2021 Maria Isabel Sánchez Vegara

Illustrations © 2021 Yelena Bryksenkova (Mary Shelley); Zafouko Yamamoto (Ada Lovelace); Pili Aguado (Harriet Tubman); Ana Sanfelippo (Emmeline Pankhurst); Frau Isa (Marie Curie); Albert Arrayas (Mahatma Gandhi); Raquel Martín (Maria Montessori); Olivia Holden (Ernest Shackleton); Anuska Allepuz (L.M. Montgomery); Ana Albero (Coco Chanel); Erica Salcedo (Georgia O'Keeffe); Elisa Munsó (Agatha Christie); Mariadiamantes (Amelia Earhart); Agathe Sorlet (Josephine Baker); Gee Fan Eng (Frida Kahlo); Linzie Hunter (Astrid Lindgren); Ashling Lindsay (Alan Turing); Marta Antelo (Rosa Parks); Anna Katharina Jansen (Jesse Owens); Bàrbara Alca (Ella Fitzgerald); Mikyo Noh (David Attenborough); Leire Salaberria (Maya Angelou); Mai Ly Degnan (Martin Luther King, Jr.); Amaia Arrazola (Audrey Hepburn); Sveta Dorosheva (Anne Frank); Ginnie Hsu (Corazon Aquino); Beatrice Cerocchi (Jane Goodall); Eleonora Arosio (Rudolf Nureyev); Amelia Flower (Wilma Rudolph); Octavia Bromell (John Lennon); Camila Rosa (Pelé); Miguel Bustos (Bruce Lee); Laura Callaghan (Vivienne Westwood); Conrad Roset (Bob Dylan); Matt Hunt (Stephen Hawking); Brosmind (Muhammad Ali); Amy Blackwell (Aretha Franklin); Miranda Sofroniou (Billie Jean King); Daria Solak (Dolly Parton); Ana Albero (David Bowie); Sophie Beer (Elton John); Asun Amar (Zaha Hadid); Lisa Koesterke (Evonne Goolagong); Aura Lewis (Steve Jobs); CACHETEJACK (Prince); Alex G Griffiths (Ayrton Senna); Luciano Lozano (Jean-Michel Basquiat); Roza Nozari (Mindy Kaling); Manal Mirza (Malala Yousafzai); Anke Weckmann (Greta Thunberg)

Original idea of the series by María Isabel Sánchez Vegara, published by Alba Editorial, S.L.U.

"Little People, BIG DREAMS" and "Pequeña & Grande" are trademarks of
Alba Editorial S.L.U. and/or Beautifool Couple S.L.

First published in the UK in 2021 by Frances Lincoln Children's Books, an imprint of The Quarto Group.
1 Triptych Place, London, SE1 9SH United Kingdom.
T (0)20 7700 6700 **www.Quarto.com**

All rights reserved.

No part of this publication may be reproduced, stored in a retrieval system, or transmitted, in any form, or by any means, electrical, mechanical, photocopying, recording or otherwise without the prior written permission of the publisher or a licence permitting restricted copying.

Any faults are the publisher's who will be happy to rectify for future printings.

A catalogue record for this book is available from the British Library.

ISBN 978-0-7112-6416-8

eBook ISBN 978-0-7112-6418-2

Set in Futura BT.

Published by Katie Cotton • Designed by Karissa Santos
Edited by Katy Flint and Lucy Menzies • Production by Nikki Ingram
Editorial Assistance from Alex Hithersay and Rachel Robinson
Additional text by Claire Saunders and Robin Pridy
Manufactured in Guangdong, China TT122024